This book is due for return on or before the
last date shown above but it may be renewed
by personal application, post, or telephone,
quoting this date and details of the book.

✿ Northamptonshire Libraries

"WHAT A LOVELY WAR!"

BRITISH SOLDIERS' SONGS

FROM THE BOER WAR
TO THE PRESENT DAY

"WHAT A LOVELY WAR!"

BRITISH SOLDIERS' SONGS

FROM THE BOER WAR
TO THE PRESENT DAY

ROY PALMER

Foreword by Lyn Macdonald

MICHAEL JOSEPH
LONDON

MICHAEL JOSEPH
Published by the Penguin Group
27 Wrights Lane, London W8 5TZ, England
Viking Penguin Inc., 375 Hudson Street, New York, NY 10014, USA
Penguin Books Australia Ltd, Ringwood, Victoria, Australia
Penguin Books Canada Ltd, 2801 John Street, Markham, Ontario, Canada L3R 1B4
Penguin Books (NZ) Ltd, 182–190 Wairau Road, Auckland 10, New Zealand

Penguin Books Ltd, Registered Offices: Harmondsworth, Middlesex, England

First published 1990

Typeset in Linotron 10½/12½ pt Ehrhardt by Cambrian Typesetters
Printed and bound in England by Clays Ltd, St Ives plc

A CIP catalogue record for this book is available
from the British Library.

ISBN 0 7181 3357 9

For Hamish Henderson

· CONTENTS ·

The Army Alphabet/xi
Foreword/1
Introduction/7

THE ARMY ALPHABET

A   Army, a part of which we're in.
B   Blooming boots, that lead us into sin.
C   Choice remarks, they use to dress us down.
D   Drill, we get until we feel quite brown.
E   Education, they try to make us learn.
F   Fatigues, we go and say it's not our turn.
G   Gong, they bang to pass the time of day.
H   Home Estab., we hope to get some day.
I   Inspections, we get by all COs.
J   Jankers, that keep us on our toes.
K   Khaki drill, mine always looks amiss.
L   Leave, we get to see our favourite miss.
M   Messing staff, who feed us all on bully.
N   No, sir, when asked if we get fed fully.
O   Orderly Room, a place that is not healthy.
P   Pay call, that's sounded for the wealthy.
Q   Quarter blokes, in front of whom we're meek.
R   Rooty gong, for which we sometimes seek.
S   Shooting, done at targets, so they say.
T   Tenderness, with which we eye our pay.
U   Uniforms, of which we have a number.
V   Vickers men, who never seem to slumber.
W   Wartime tales, they tell to all recruits.
X   Extra pay, we get for doing TEWTs.
Y   Youngest sub., who once in civvies stood.
Z   Zenith of the alphabet so good.

· FOREWORD ·

IT HAS BEEN MY pleasure to have had some slight connection with this book since Roy Palmer wrote to ask permission to use some of the songs which appeared in my own books and this led to a lively and, to me at least, enjoyable correspondence – although I half suspect that, as I pressed more and more songs of the Great War on the author's attention, it might have been less so to him! For his intention was to cover a wider spectrum than the conflict which has absorbed my own professional interest for the past sixteen years.

Before that time I was unfamiliar with soldiers' songs – apart from a general familiarity with ditties of the popular-sing-song variety like 'Tipperary'. 'Tipperary' is commonly regarded as being *the* song of the First World War. It has a catchy tune; it had been the hit song of 1913 and, in those days before the advent of electronic mass-entertainment, its appeal had by no means worn out a year later when the first of a great cavalcade of British soldiers marched towards Mons and the first of the great battles of what was to be the Great War. Those soldiers certainly sang it and the circumstances caught the popular imagination and made the song immortal. But 'Tipperary' was a 'soldiers' song' only briefly and by association. It was as remote from the experience of the First World War trenches as two decades later the anodyne sentiments of 'The White Cliffs of Dover' would be from the experience of sweltering in the desert or being bombed and machine-gunned on the beaches of Normandy. Jimmy, like all those other 'Jimmies' who went before or would come after, was thinking not so much of the day when he would 'go to sleep in his own little room again' as of emerging unscathed from the battle, of the next beer, the next decent meal, the next 'bird' to be chatted up. Great War Songs, yes. But soldiers' songs? Never! ('A long way to Tipperary' soon descended on the lips of the soldiers to a parody of which the only printable lines were 'That's the wrong way to tickle Mary, it's the wrong way you know' . . .)

I first heard real soldiers' songs – and soldiers singing them – at the end of a day of pilgrimage. The coachload of Old Soldiers had been touring the battlefields round Arras and Ypres, visiting cemeteries, paying tribute at monuments, laying wreaths, planting crosses on individual graves. It had been a solemn day, almost an awesome experience for an outsider to watch and listen as these veterans recalled bitter times, remembering mates who had 'gone west', or standing in silent contemplation of some apparently innocent stretch of farmland. They were still silent and taciturn on the road back. And then there was a shout from the back of the coach. 'Cor! Look boys! There's that old estaminet at the crossroads. Fancy it still being there!'

That broke the tension. In a moment the coach was buzzing with cheerful chatter. Then old Fred White leaped up from his seat, whipped out his mouth organ (and also his dentures the better to play it) and they began to sing.

They also laughed, and whistled and cheered, joining in one irreverent ditty after another. The tunes were familiar. The words were not – and many of the fruitier choruses trailed off in abashed chuckles as the tolerant smiles of their wives became a trifle fixed.

It was the start of my affection for soldiers' songs – and it was the birth of the realization, vital to an historian, that songs are as much a part of soldiering as battles and gallantry and endurance. They are the safety valve, the means of letting off steam which makes it possible to put up with the discipline, the strictures of army life, the loss of individuality – even (and perhaps most of all) the brutalizing horrors of battle. It was easy then to understand how young men could march away from some decimating experience in the trenches and were able only hours later to drink and joke and raise the roof – and the bawdier the songs the better. Sixty years later at the end of a day heavy with mourning, as their coach drove along the Flanders roads they had once so painfully marched, they were doing exactly the same thing. It was a useful lesson and one which prompted me ever afterwards when talking to Old Soldiers about their experiences to ask, 'What songs did you sing?' Frequently the replies have been illuminating.

Roy Palmer has firmly laid to rest the myth that the Second World War produced no memorable soldiers' songs 'because it wasn't a marching war', but inevitably the songs are different in style, if not in character, and part of the interest of this collection is in the tunes which different generations of soldiers have parodied. If the words are revealing about life in the army, so the tunes reflect the culture of the society that army served.

In the First World War, or Everyman's War, when at one point the British Army contained more than five million men – most of them civilians masquerading as soldiers – when the Churches were the pillars of society and formal religious observance was an accepted fact of life, every schoolchild's day began and ended with prayers and hymn-singing, the best part of every Sunday was spent in church or chapel, and the only affordable leisure entertainment was provided by church organizations like the temperance Band of Hope and the Boys' Brigade. It is hardly surprising if the Tommy of the First World War appropriated these so-familiar hymn tunes for less reverent ends. There was a tacit understanding that they had a 'fool's licence', and it must have relieved the rebellious spirit chafing at the bit of army discipline to express in anti-authoritarian song the scurrilous insubordinate sentiments that would have sent a soldier smartly to clink if he had expressed them directly in the hearing of an officer. In much the same way jesters of old must have bandied insults that, without the protection of cap and bells, would have landed them in a dungeon.

With only a few exceptions (which, perhaps significantly, date from the flog-'em-and-hang-'em era), it is striking that there is remarkably little bitterness, and such as there is couched in irony that is not without humour.

One example is 'D-Day Dodgers' – the anthem of hard-fighting troops in Italy in 1944 who were sneered at for dodging the 'real' war in France – surprisingly similar to a sideswipe at civilians in a song sung by the troops in Salonika almost thirty years before:

> It seems that the people at home there,
> When they talk about things in the war,
> Think the Balkan stunt only a side show,
> And sneer at us lads, and what's more
> They tell us our life here is rosy,
> We're out on a holiday trip,
> And perhaps you agree; if that's so, mate,
> Just listen to us for a bit . . .

My own collection of songs and ephemera of the First World War contains one gem which points up the yawning gulf between the attitudes of soldiers and those of well-meaning civilians. Early in the war a gentleman by the name of A.C. Ainger 'did his bit' by producing a booklet of *Marching Songs for Soldiers set to well-known tunes* which could have served no useful purpose other than providing the soldiers with a good laugh. It's all too easy to imagine the words *they* might have composed to parody 'Here's to the Maiden of Bashful Fifteen'. Their minds would hardly have run on the lines of Mr Ainger's:

> Here's to the health of the King and the Queen,
> Ever at work for a living,
> Morning and evening and all that's between
> Cheering and helping and giving –
> Give them a shout,
> Lengthen it out,
> Tell friends and enemies what we're about!

Despite huge sales to enthusiastic relatives who lovingly despatched them to their boys in France, it's unlikely that the roads they marched ever rang to the sound of that or any other of Ainger's compositions, though one of them did become popular on the home front:

> Tramp, tramp, tramp the boys are marching,
> Cheer up, comrades, we will come,
> And beneath the Union Jack
> We will drive the Germans back,
> For the safety of our own beloved home.

One can almost hear the howls of derision with which the troops in France would have shouted *that* one down, for what is markedly missing in the genuine soldiers' songs is 'patriotism' in the sense in which it was understood and promoted at Home. No matter how they felt it – and in view of the number of volunteers who served in both wars they must have felt it to a degree – one gets the feeling that patriotism was a sentiment which British soldiers found vaguely embarrassing. The Second World War produced the story of two shot-down fliers who were rescued and sheltered by the Maquis in a remote mountain hide-out in occupied France. At the end of one campfire sing-song which had whiled away a chilly evening, their throats lubricated by much red wine, the Frenchmen gave a tearful rendering of the Marseillaise and invited their allies to riposte with *their* National Anthem. It may not have enhanced the reputation of the RAF but two of its members had the exquisite satisfaction of seeing the Frenchmen stand respectfully to attention as, with equal solemnity, they boomed to the tune of 'Hark the Herald Angels Sing':

> Uncle George and Auntie Mabel
> Fainted at the breakfast table.
> Which should be an awful warning
> Not to do it in the morning.
> But Ovaltine has put them right,
> Now they do it morn and night.
> And Uncle George is hoping soon
> To do it in the afternoon.

Such lewdness was mild by comparison with some songs which are rightly included in this book. But, in the case of most of the singers, the crudity owed more to the traditional bravado of schoolboy smut than to lascivious personal experience in the ranks of the 'rude and licentious soldiery'. We live in less puritanical times, but in the First World War – and possibly also in the Second – boys coming into the ranks fresh from school and the bosoms of respectable families were secretly shocked by the blatant obscenity of the songs that were sung as a matter of course in the ranks. (I know of at least one, now in his nineties, who still is!) But their blushes soon faded; it was a greater shame, after all, to be scorned as a wimp or a weakling. And there was safety in numbers; a licence in comradeship. It is a youthful point of view, but it is important to remember that wars are fought by young men – or, at least, by men who are young in years. One soldier from New Zealand, where conscription was never introduced, once tellingly described to me his return home in 1919 after four years' soldiering:

> You can imagine how eager I was to get back to the homefolks and civilian life – longing for it. One of the things I'd really looked forward to was getting back to the cricket club and seeing some of my old chums again. I went down the first Saturday I was home, but I only went once more after that. I had nothing to say to the other fellows. They were the same age as me, twenty-three. But they were boys. I was an old man.

The experiences of the front-line soldiers made old men of them all. It is that experience of war which comes through in the songs the soldiers sang, not in bellicose description or sad recollection of lost comrades but unexpectedly, as in two lines of the mournful dirge 'I Want to Go Home':

> . . . take me over the sea, Where the Alleyman can't get at me . . .

'Alleyman', of course, was a corruption of the French 'Allemand', meaning 'German', but the Tommy's interpretation conjures up a chilling vision that says as much about the real fear and dread that every soldier felt and few dared express, than a dozen descriptive passages of purple prose.

This foreword has dwelt disproportionately on the First World War, but I make no apology, for a common thread runs through all soldiers' songs. To read this collection is to realize that there is not so much difference between the soldier shivering in the Flanders mud in Marlborough's wars in the eighteenth century and the soldiers who struggled through the same mud to Passchendaele in the twentieth, sticking it out as later generations of soldiers would stick it out, slogging from Normandy to the Ardennes, or yomping across the tundras of the Falklands.

Lyn Macdonald
London, 1990

INTRODUCTION

Military Music

'Every horseman at the fyrst blaste of the trumpette shall sadle or cause to be sadled his horse, at the seconde to brydell, at the thirde to leape on his horsebacke, to wait on the kyng, or his lorde or capitayne'; so runs part of the *Rules and Ordynaunces for the Warre*, of 1544.[1] Instructions were given to soldiers by call of trumpet or beat of drum for centuries, and even when the practice was superseded in battle it continued in normal routine. Until well within living memory the soldier's daily timetable, from reveille to lights out, was punctuated by bugle or bagpipe.

The music of military bands, which also has a long history, comes to the ear of the civilian through televised ceremonies such as Trooping the Colour on the Queen's Birthday or the Remembrance Day parades. Marching soldiers, both in peace and war, were often heartened by bands playing the familiar tunes of their regiments.

A third component of military music is (or was) hymns. When church parades were routine and compulsory, even in the field, the melodies of certain hymns such as 'Onward, Christian Soldiers' were regularly impressed on the memories of servicemen.

Now, all these types of official military music were appropriated by soldiers for their own purposes. Bugle calls had words put to them which were intended sometimes merely to help men remember what was being signalled, sometimes to add pointed or humorous comment. The reveille call was given this lyric in the Wiltshire Regiment:

> Get out of bed, get out of bed,
> You lazy buggers.
> I feel sorry for you, I do.[2]

A summons to the parade ground was more neutral:

> Fall in A, fall in B,
> Fall in every company.[3]

On the other hand, the news of 'No Parade' or 'Dismiss' caused undisguised glee:

> There's no parade today, there's no parade today.
> The adjutant's got a bellyache and the colonel's gone away.[4]

The announcement of the men's meal was welcomed ('Come to the cookhouse door, boys, Come to the cookhouse door'[5]) but that of the officers elicited this response:

> The officers' wives get puddens and pies;
> A sergeant's wife gets skilly.
> A private's wife gets nothing at all
> To fill her empty belly.[6]

Resentment against officers was expressed also in these words, sung, of course, by the men, to the tune of the officers' call:

> Officers come and be damned,
> Officers come and be damned,
> Officers come and be damned,
> Damned, damned, damned.[7]

A given call had its variations in unofficial words from regiment to regiment. The Royal Dragoons were summoned to feed their horses in this way, or rather these words went through their minds when they heard the call:

> Come to the stable all ye that are able,
> And give your fine horses their water and corn.[8]

The Royal Field Artillery, with a more extended piece of bugling, had:

> Come to the stable you men that are able,
> And feed up your horses with water and corn,
> Feed up your horses with water and corn.
> Don't give 'em too much or you'll wish you'd not been born.
> Come to the stable you men that are able,
> And feed up your horses with water and corn.[9]

The same regiment had ironic but good-natured words to accompany the summons to pay parade:

> Oh come and get your pay, oh come and get your pay.
> The sergeant-major's got some money and wants to give it away.[10]

Kipling's poem, 'Route Marchin' ', describes striking camp, and then beginning the day's march: 'Oh, then it's open order, an' we lights our pipes and sings'.[11] A lesser poet, Patrick MacGill, fought in the First World War himself. In 'The Return' he evokes a tired and dejected detachment of soldiers pulling out of the line in the morning, and suddenly having their spirits lifted by a snatch of song:

> Back again from the battle,
> From the mates we've left behind,
> And our officers are gloomy
> And the NCOs are kind;
> When a Jew's harp breaks the silence,
> Purring an old refrain,
> Singing the song of the soldier,
> 'Here we are again!'[12]

Again and again one finds such comments, especially during the First World War. Edmund Blunden recalled 'passing Albert with songs', and how his battalion marched 'singing towards the Somme'.[13] Robert Graves, to choose one reference from many, writes in *Goodbye to All That*:

> That night we marched back again to Cambrin. The men were singing. Being mostly from the Midlands, they sang comic songs rather than Welsh hymns: 'Slippery Sam', 'When we've Wound up the Watch on the Rhine', and 'I do like a S'nice S'mince Pie', to concertina accompaniment.[14]

George Coppard, who added three to his sixteen years of age so as to join the Royal West Surrey Regiment in 1914, remembers the pains and pleasures of marching in France:

> As we marched our spirits soared, in spite of our 80-pound load . . . To the sound of mouth-organs playing, the marching column would break into song, each platoon or company singing a different tune perhaps. 'Colonel Bogey' was second only to lowbrow rhymes about the war, sung to well-known hymn tunes with words varied to taste.[15]

Unofficial words to the tunes of military marches were seldom written down, because they were disrespectful or obscene, or both. George Hall was on the retreat from Mons in 1914 with the Second Battalion of the Royal Sussex Regiment. When the few weary survivors finally stumbled back behind their lines they were welcomed by a band that struck up the regimental march, 'Sussex by the Sea'. To a man, the soldiers joined in, but with these words:

> Good old Sussex by the sea, I've shit 'em,
> Dear old Sussex by the sea, I've shit 'em.
> You can tell them all that they know fuck all
> In Sussex by the sea.[16]

General Haig, who shortly afterwards became Commander-in-Chief of the British Army, took particular exception to such singing. As Lyn Macdonald points out, 'No battalion would have ventured to march to a ribald song within miles of his headquarters.'[17] However, a column of men, unaware of Haig's presence, happened to pass in full voice through a village in which he was conducting an inspection. When he heard:

> Do your balls hang low?
> Do they dangle to and fro?
> Can you tie them in a knot?
> Can you tie them in a bow?

he called for his horse, and set off in pursuit, with the intention of speaking to the colonel who was riding at the head of the battalion. As Haig drew level with platoon after platoon, each fell silent. Eventually, the colonel alone sang on, oblivious, and had just delivered the words:

> Can you sling them on your shoulder
> Like a lousy fucking soldier?
> Do your balls hang low?

when the Commander-in-Chief caught up. A whispered conversation ensued, which included Haig's ruling: 'I like the tune, but the words are inexcusable.'[18]

There is no doubt that he would have felt the same about this lyric, to the tune of Sousa's march, 'Blaze Away':

> Twenty-one, never been done,
> Queen of all the virgins.
> Ain't it a pity she'd only one titty
> To feed the baby on?
> I'm ever so sorry a bloody big lorry
> Ran over the other one.
> Oh all of a frolic a dirty big ballock
> Came sailing through the air.
> It circled once and on the nonce
> It hit me in the hair.
>
> As he grew older and bolder
> He took himself in hand,
> Left and right with all his might
> To the tune of an army band.
> Oh she was a cripple with only one nipple
> To feed the baby on.
> Poor little fucker, he'd only one sucker
> To start his life upon.[19]

Sometimes the unofficial lyric was limited to just a few words. Coppard's 'Colonel Bogey', for example, which was 'probably the most frequently heard march-tune in the British Army'[20] during the First World War, consisted merely of the words, 'Ballocks, and the same to you'. Sometimes, as with the song encountered by General Haig, there were several verses.

The hymn tunes adopted by soldiers for their own use were in some cases remembered from childhood. 'We are but little children weak', which became 'We Are but Little Seaforths weak',* is (or was) in *The Methodist School Hymnal*. Others were heard again and again at the church parades which were regularly held. Frank Richards, who served through the First World War in the Royal Welch Regiment, wrote:

> We had a mouth-organ band who used to play the hymns: we liked the tunes of some of the hymns, but not the words. We preferred our own words which we set to the tune and sang with great gusto when we were having a jollification. These words, set to the tune of 'O God, Our Help in Ages Past', were a great favourite among us:
>
> > John Wesley had a little dog, he was so very thin.
> > He took him to the Gates of Hell and threw the bastard in.[21]

Soldiers' words sometimes directly parodied those of the original hymn, which means that part of their impact lay in the tension set up between the old and the new.

---

* Songs asterisked in the Introduction appear in the text.

'Holy, holy, holy', for example, became 'Grousing, grousing, grousing'.* There is a moving scene in the film version of *Oh, What a Lovely War!* when the singing of serried ranks of church-parading soldiers dissolves surrealistically from 'The Church's One Foundation' to 'We Are Fred Karno's Army'.* In this case, the words bear no relationship to the original except a shared metre and tune, but there was no doubt a delight in incongruity and in irreligious relish when using a sacred tune for secular, not to say scurrilous matter. Frank Richards' 'John Wesley' illustrates this too; so does 'Shari Wag El Burka'* from the Second World War, an account of a visit to a brothel sung to the tune of 'Onward, Christian Soldiers'.

Singing on the march was a semi-official activity in that it was, within limits, permitted or condoned by military authority or practice. The same was true of concert parties arranged by battalions, regiments, or even armies. One such was filmed aboard the *QE2* in 1983 as she sailed towards the Falklands. Soldiers were singing, among other things, a lyric including the words, 'I'm going to get me a Spic or two'.

Much the same spirit seems to have prevailed at a divisional concert held in France in 1916 near Senlis when, according to Edmund Blunden, the musical fare included 'Take me back to dear old Blighty', 'Mr Bottomley – good old Horatio', 'When you're a long, long way from home', and:

> When you're deep in a decline
> Who provides the Number Nine?
> Mr Bottomley – John Bull.[22]

Again, at the beginning of the Second World War, Stan McMahon, who served in the Royal Engineers, the African Pioneers and the Pioneer Corps, remembers that his first night in the army was marked by a camp concert, which included 'Roll out the Barrel', 'Little Sir Echo' and 'There'll always be an England'. In France he heard 'We'll hang out the washing on the Siegfried Line', and, back in England, waiting to go to the Middle East, 'Begin the Beguine' and 'Wish me luck as you wave me goodbye', the latter from Gracie Fields. 'On the rare occasions when there was any kind of communal singing,' he writes, 'it was the old favourites, "Tipperary", "Pack Up your Troubles", "Show Me the Way to Go Home".'[23]

All these were of commercial and civilian origin, but soldiers' own compositions might find a place at concert parties provided they did not go beyond certain limits. 'South of Meiktila',* for example, celebrates a successful engagement in Burma. It was written by a Sergeant Tommy Wren of the Border Regiment, and sung at a battalion concert party at Waw, near the Sittang River, in September 1945.

The Unofficial Repertoire

Not surprisingly, the repertoire was much more wide-ranging on completely informal and unofficial occasions. On troopships or in barrack rooms, songs 'were sung by odd people at odd times, and others took them up'.[24] Blunden remembered at Croix Barbée in 1916 'a spontaneous concert by the company signallers, who, sitting in the twilight under a cherry-tree, sang such rude old masterpieces as "The Ram of Derby" with irresistible spirit.'[25]

During the Spanish Civil War, J. H. Bassett, who was fighting on the republican side, recalled:

> One evening, we were sitting along the kerb of the main street waiting for the cinema to open. The men began to sing, in every language. The British sang, 'There's a valley in Spain called Jarama'* and 'No Pasarán' and 'We came to sunny Spain to make the people smile again, And to chase the fascist bastards over hill and over plain'.[26]

Others in Spain, British veterans of the First World War, sang 'The Quartermaster Stores'* and 'Tipperary'. (F. T. Nettleingham, an early anthologist of songs from the First World War, says the latter was 'never Tommy's song . . . never greatly sung',[27] yet it was often mentioned and frequently parodied.)

During the prolonged periods soldiers spent in the trenches of the First World War singing was an important recreation, and indeed more than a recreation:

> It's a funny thing, but when you get frightened someone starts a song and you all yell it out. It's a sort of bravado affair. So we lay there in that ditch with the shells falling round, and we were singing for all we were worth. We were singing 'Ragtime Cowboy Joe', and I never hear that song but I think of us lying there and those guns banging away and those shells exploding.[28]

George Coppard, who also recalled concert parties immediately behind the lines, said that singing in the trenches was 'very important, and there were some who were outstandingly favoured because of their ability to sing. Every soldier, including myself, tried to get the words off'. When he was asked whether songs like 'Tipperary' and 'Roses of Picardy' were as popular in the trenches as is now believed, he replied:

> Not so much as those which suggest something spicy. What you've got to think, I suppose, is that all the troops were just men. It's natural that here's an opportunity where you can say whatever you like in a song. There's no girl to say it's terrible or something like that, so you can get on with it, and that gives you a good laugh.[29]

The repertoire was probably very similar to that of the 'sods' operas', beery sing-songs which took place in all three services. In the case of the army, the lower ranks used the barrack room or wet canteen, the sergeants their mess. Stan McMahon recalls rugby songs like 'The Highland Tinker' and 'Hitler's only got one ball'. Surprisingly, perhaps, there were also sentimental ballads like 'Comrades, comrades, ever since we were boys' and 'Nelly Dean'. This reminds one of Nettleingham's remark that during the First World War 'Annie Laurie' was 'the most popular and often sung':

> I have heard 'Annie Laurie' in peace and war; at home and abroad; in camp and on the march; in a big dining hall with 300 men and no dinner . . . The only other tune that approaches it in popularity . . . is the harmonised version of 'Home, Sweet Home'.[30]

In the wet canteen, especially on pay day, sing-songs were frequent, at least in the experience of some soldiers. Bob Copper, who comes from a noted Sussex family of singers, was in the Life Guards in the 1930s. He notes with some disappointment:

> The songs I remember singing in the barrack room or canteen were Bing Crosby hits and the like, learnt from the radio . . . In the stables you would sometimes hear a line or two . . . mostly parodies with tunes from what I should think are old hymns.

He quotes snatches from 'When this bloody war is over',* 'If I had the wings of an angel', 'She was poor but she was honest' and 'I took my girl for a ramble'.[31]

Tom Langley, a Blackcountryman, was in the Grenadier Guards a little earlier, from 1924 to 1927. He remembered:

> In those days there was always a canteen king, an old soldier, often with a passable voice. The king was accepted as an authority on all things military. He reminisced endlessly of his early days in the regiment when Aldershot was a bell tent and 'Slope pikes' was the order on Buckingham Palace guard. He would always oblige with a song and accept a pint. The particular king I recall had about 25 years' service. His wife did the company washing, and during the day he marched around the ablutions with a polishing cloth in his hand. No one ever saw him polish anything. According to him the colonel did not know he was in the regiment until he applied to extend his service beyond 21 years.[32]

John Gregson of Burnley, who joined the Royal Field Artillery and went to India in 1929, heard and learnt many songs at 'boozy singing sessions' held in wet canteens. On occasions, those present were obliged, in the time-honoured formula, to 'sing, say, pay or show your arse'. When the canteen closed the session would often continue in the riding school.

For preference, songs dealt with 'some heroic deed' or were sentimental or 'bawdily humorous'. Those critical of the army were especially appreciated: 'if you're doing seven years at two bob a day you like to cock a snook'.[33] Several of Gregson's songs are given below, including 'Kevin Barry', 'Merry Battery Boys' and 'Orderly Man'.

Harold Wirdnam joined the Wiltshire Regiment in 1934, and served for eight years in India from 1936. The songs he learnt in the barrack room, in the wet canteen and on the march are an extraordinary mixture. There are highly serious items like 'Scotland the Brave', 'The British Grenadiers' and 'Those in Peril on the Sea'. Jolly songs like 'Blaydon Races' and 'Alexander's Ragtime Band' alternate with sentimental ballads like 'Sweethearts and Wives'. A number of traditional Irish songs include 'The Boston Burglar' and 'McCaffery'.* While Wirdnam, like all soldiers of his time, immediately points out that the latter was 'taboo' (officially, that is), he surprisingly adds that soldiers freely sang 'Off to Dublin in the Green', an IRA adaptation of a gung-ho recruiting song. Finally, he sang the universally known 'Bless 'em All'* and 'Old King Cole'.[34]

'Old King Cole' is also part of the repertoire of Gordon Hall, from another Sussex family of singers. He sang it himself as a national serviceman in the early fifties; his oldest brother sang it in the Second World War; their father sang it in the

First. The family's contribution goes far beyond that. Gordon's uncle, Fred, served for twenty years in India and spent part of the First World War in Germany as a prisoner-of-war. He was a keen monologist, but also sang his own version of 'McCaffery',* under the title of 'Preston Barracks'.

Gordon's mother, Mabel, who is still alive, worked for the NACB (Navy and Army Catering Board, a forerunner of the NAAFI) at Crowborough Camp in 1916, and learnt there a huge number of soldiers' favourite songs, from 'Mademoiselle from Armentières' to 'Break the News to Mother',* and from 'The Baby's Name will be Kitchener' to 'Take me back to dear old Blighty'. Gordon himself did national service in the Royal Artillery in the early 1950s. He sang in NAAFI canteens from Oswestry to Ismailia, in local pubs, on troopships, and even (when opportunities presented themselves) while confined in the unit guardroom. From his time in Egypt he remembers a twenty-five-mile route march by the Suez Canal when weary feet were galvanised by an old sergeant's breaking into 'Tipperary'.

Sessions in the NAAFI at a camp near Ismailia would have been immediately familiar, with the exception of a song or two, to generations of soldiers. The repertoire, catholic as ever, included touching songs like 'Ave Maria' and 'Ramona'. American sources yielded 'Old Man River', 'Buddy, can you spare a dime?' and 'Hallelujah, I'm a bum'. A Scots soldier favoured 'We're no awa to bide awa', and this was picked up by the rest. An Irishman contributed 'Kevin Barry'.* The scurrilous vein was represented by 'Oh, up in Akaba' and by 'King Farouk', which Gordon Hall describes as 'the most popular song of the Second World War'.[35]

The Old Tradition and New Songs

The old tradition of army singing was still very much alive, then, until at least the 1950s. The songs can be categorised in many different ways. In terms of function, there were songs for marching and songs for relaxation, though the distinction is far from absolute. Brophy and Partridge, dealing with the repertoire of the 1914–18 War, differentiate between 'songs predominantly sung on the march', 'songs sung on the march, but more often in billets and *estaminets*' and 'chants and songs rarely, if ever, sung on the march'.[36] Nettleingham, on the same period, distinguishes only between 'route and marching' and 'camp or concert' songs.[37]

In terms of origin, one could attempt to separate military and civilian songs, though civilians learnt some military songs ('Bless 'em All', for example), and soldiers not only sang civilian songs but did not hesitate to adapt them for their own purposes. A recruit would inevitably bring with him a repertoire acquired at home or work, in a public house or music hall. If he came from a family or community rich in traditional song his repertoire would naturally reflect this. Ivor Gurney, the musician and poet who enlisted in 1915 as a private in the Gloucestershire Regiment, wrote of a fellow soldier called Fred Bennett:

> I have discovered a delightful creature. A great broad chested heavy chap who has been a morris dancer and whose fathers and grandfathers, uncles and other relations know all the folk songs imaginable. High Germanie, High Barbarie, O No John, I'm Seventeen Come Sunday – whole piles of 'em . . . He whistled 'Constant Billy' which I have never heard before.[38]

Men from communities in which traditional songs had been eclipsed – and these were no doubt in the majority by the time of the Second World War – brought the popular songs of the day, learnt from sheet music, the music hall, or, latterly, records and radio. For example, 'South of the Border', written in 1939 by Jimmy Kennedy and Michael Carr, immediately became popular on both sides of the Atlantic through broadcasts. Soldiers of the British Expeditionary Force sang it in France in 1940 in its original form, but the tune remained well enough known five years later to serve as a vehicle for 'South of Meiktila'.* This seems to have been confined to a particular unit, but other soldier-made songs spread. 'D-Day Dodgers',* to the tune of 'Lili Marlene', became more or less the universal property of British and North American soldiers who served in Italy in 1944 and 1945 (and I have also heard of, but not traced, a version dealing retrospectively with the North African campaigns of 1942 and 1943).

The creation of a song by one hand or many, and its adoption, variation and communal transmisson, typify classic folk song. Brophy and Partridge wrote that soldiers' songs 'are genuine folk-songs . . . They come from the ranks, especially from the private soldiers without ambition to bear office or social responsibility'.[39] J. B. Priestley used the same term for the songs he heard during his own service in the First World War. In *Margin Released* he quotes part of a song of 1914 ('We don't want to lose you But we think you ought to go, For your king and country Both need you so'), then comments:

> The First World War, unlike the Second, produced two distinct crops of songs: one for patriotic civilians, like that drivel above; the other, not composed and copyrighted by anybody, genuine folk song, for the sardonic front-line troops.

He goes on to list three types of these 'genuine folk songs': 'bawdy', 'lugubrious and homesick, without patriotic sentiment of any kind', and those 'sharply concerned with military life from the point of view of the disillusioned private'.[40]

Patrick MacGill was also intrigued by the front-line repertoire:

> The soldiers have songs of their own, songs of the march, the trench, the billet and battle. Their origin is lost; the songs have arisen like old folk-tales, spontaneous choruses that voice the moods of a moment and of many moments which are monotonously alike.[41]

Much as he admired these soldiers' songs, though, he believed that 'none will outlast the turmoil in which they originated; having weathered the leaden storms of war, their vibrant strains will be choked and smothered in atmospheres of peace'.

Or, putting it in the words of his friend, Rifleman Bill Teake: 'These 'ere songs are no good in England. They 'ave too much guts in them.'[42]

In fact, many of the soldiers' songs of the First World War did survive the peace. Some even became known to civilians in England. Some were passed on to new generations of soldiers. In addition, all the categories of song mentioned by Priestley and MacGill flourished in the Second World War. There were major differences, of course, one of which was the existence of radio. Soldiers were kept in much closer touch with official thinking and with the musical culture of home, and the strength of their own sub-culture was potentially lessened.

As Hamish Henderson puts it, 'the balladry of World War II . . . grew up under the shadow of – and often in virtual conflict with – the official or commercial radio of the combatant nations'. He adds:

> The state radio in time of war does not encourage divergence from the straight patriotic line. It regards most expressions of the human reaction to soldiering as a drag on the national war effort. Accordingly, it does not allot a great deal of time to the genuine army ballad. For the army balladeer comes of a rebellious house. His characteristic tone is one of cynicism. The aims of his government and the military virtue of his comrades are alike target for unsparing (and usually obscene) comment. Shakespeare, who ran God close in the matter of creation, knew him well and called him Thersites. Of course, the state radio was wrong about the morale effect of the army ballad, as about nearly everything else. Perhaps the most cynical ballads of the war were produced by German troops in Italy as the same time they were fighting an exemplary rearguard action right up the peninsula.[43]

The cynicism and obscenity of many soldiers' songs have inevitably led to difficulties over their appearance in print. Snatches quoted in the many memoirs of the First World War are usually bowdlerised. An honourable exception is Frederic Manning's autobiographical novel, *The Middle Parts of Fortune*, which mentions songs like ' 'Ere we go again', 'Cock Robin' and 'I want to go 'ome'.* When quoting one fragment, to the tune of the 'Marseillaise', Manning disguises the name of the regiment (in fact, the Shropshires), but not the language:

> At la Clytte, at la Clytte,
> Where the Westshires got well beat,
> And the bullets blew our buttons all away,
> And we ran, yes, we ran,
> From that fuckin' Alleman;
> And now we are happy all the day.[44]

On another occasion, he reports,

> the marching column broke into a cheerful song. They had put, at least partially, their own words to the air of a song sufficiently sentimental:

> > Oh, they've called them up from Westchurch,
> > And they've called them up from Wem,
> > And they'll call up all the women
> > When they've fucked up all the men.[45]

Another time, he tells how soldiers flock into an *estaminet* after being paid, and stamp in time on the floor as they sing at the tops of their voices:

> Mademoiselle, she bought a cow, parley-voo.
> To milk the brute she didn't know how, parley-voo.
> She pulled the tail instead of the tit,
> And covered herself all over with milk,
> Inky pinky, parley-voo.[46]

Examples such as this very much bear out Lyn Macdonald's conclusion that there was a 'bawdy free-masonry' in the ranks, and also, perhaps, that 'there was a verse-smith in most battalions'.[47] Anthologists have often been reluctant fully to reflect such things.

Many collections are timid, though allowances have to be made for the canons of taste prevailing when they appeared. The earliest volumes to publish the vernacular songs of twentieth-century soldiers were *Tommy's Tunes* and *More Tommy's Tunes*, edited respectively in 1917 and 1918 by Second-Lieutenant F. T. Nettleingham of the Royal Flying Corps. These are invaluable, especially as they include music, but they expurgate many songs and omit others, including, as Nettleingham admits, 'a large number of the wittiest – albeit, of a coarse kind – the gayest – as regards tune – and most frequently sung – therefore popular – creations [which] are so untranslatable as to render them unprintable for popular consumption'.[48]

In 1930, objecting to the 'unnecessary bowdlerisation' which they had found when songs were quoted in 'war books', Brophy and Partridge in *Songs and Slang of the British Soldier, 1914–18*, set out 'to secure completeness', but themselves jibbed at including the 'three very ugly words around which almost all army obscenities revolved'.[49] In the same year, a probably wider readership was reached by *Songs that Won the War*, edited by S. Louis Giraud for the *Daily Express*, and issued as its *Community Song Book, No. 3*. This covered both 'Published Songs Popular During the War', such as 'Tipperary' and 'Pack Up Your Troubles', and 'Songs Composed and Parodied by the Soldiers', such as 'I Want to Go Home'* and 'Never Mind'.* The language is chaste. Every 'bloody' is changed to 'bally' or 'rotten'. Songs and allusions of a sexual nature do not feature at all, and at one point even the horror is masked when 'if you get stuck on the wire' is replaced by the curious 'if you get stuck on the mire'.[50] The volume nevertheless introduced civilians to part of the soldiers' repertoire, and no doubt elicited many a chuckle from veterans as they were reminded of earthier versions of some of the words.

After the Second World War there was no new *Songs that Won the War*, interesting though such a work might have been. The pioneer was Hamish Henderson, poet of *Elegies for the Dead in Cyrenaica* (1948), and veteran of the Italian campaign.[51] *Ballads of World War II*, a slim and now extremely rare volume published circa 1950, includes both his own and others' work. 'Needless to say', he writes, 'I have refused to insult these ballads by bowdlerising them.'[52] The same approach was taken by Martin Page in the two collections he published in the 1970s,[53] bringing coverage up to the 1950s and national service. I have also adopted it in the present book.

The End of an Era

The period covered runs in fact from the Zulu War for about a hundred years, to the 1970s and 1980s. Of roughly 120 songs, some are epigrammatic, while others run to many verses. Documentary sources – archives and the printed page – account for about a third of the material. The remainder comes, directly or indirectly (and mostly the former), from oral tradition. To be more precise, from my own recordings of old soldiers or their families and friends, or from similar recordings generously communicated by others.

Some twenty-five of the songs have not, to the best of my knowledge, previously appeared in book form. In addition, many others are given here in variants which are previously unpublished. Conversely, some very well-known songs like 'Tipperary' and 'Roll out the Barrel' have been omitted precisely because they are so familiar.

As recently as 1987 I heard a number of the songs here, including 'Bless 'em All', 'Paratrooper's Song' and 'The Quartermaster Stores', sung by ex-soldiers in the public bar of a Wiltshire pub. It would not have been difficult to repeat the experience many times over in different places. Whether such songs are still sung by serving soldiers is a different question. Since the ending of national service in 1963 only volunteers have served, and after basic training they spend a good deal of their time in normal family and community life. Comradeship is still there, but the cramped culture of barrack room and the rough humour of marching column are now perhaps the exception rather than the rule. Professional soldiers tend to be pro-establishment, which is why the Falklands War and the Northern Ireland troubles appear to have produced no songs – in the army, that is.

In the South Atlantic a longer war and a mass participation of the unwilling and the disenchanted – not for a moment that I would want these things – might have rekindled the old creative fires. In Northern Ireland, one song written in 1972 by a professional songwriter, Harvey Andrews, has become very widely known among soldiers, and at the same time divorced in classic folk-song style from its author. 'Soldier',* Andrews' song, might conceivably rub shoulders with other pieces made by soldiers themselves. If so, I should be interested to discover them. It would be very sad if we had seen the end of the 'rhymes and tunes of Tommy himself', of 'the hidden well whence springs his indomitable endurance, his dogged tenacity, his superb heroism';[54] and, one might add, of his magnificent sense of humour, his acerbic wit, and his sense of justice and fair play.

These songs, with their huge variety of treatment, attitude and subject matter, combine to provide a vivid reflection of the preoccupations of British soldiers, in war and peace, at home and abroad, over a period of a century, from the 1870s to the present day. They are valuable social documents, which can be read alongside the historical record, and also the literary canon, from Robert Graves to Henry Williamson in the First World War and from Henry Reed to Raleigh Trevelyan in the Second.

The viewpoint is very much that of the lower ranks, and the songs, as Gavin Greig remarked of those from the French and Napoleonic Wars, contain 'things that are not to be found in despatches'.[55] Yet they are much more than mere documentation. They have a powerful emotional charge which still impresses, shocks, delights, persuades. They have a message, too, which, taken as a whole, directly derives from soldiers' experience and is profoundly anti-militarist.

While working on this book I was asked by a radio interviewer whether it might not foster an unhealthy interest in war. My answer was, and is, that the proper study of war can help the just desire for peace.

Roy Palmer
October 1990

· CHAPTER ONE ·

JOINING

KIT INSPECTION

You all know that terrible feeling
When your socks are out of repair,
And you ain't got no laces or blacking,
Nor a hairbrush for doing your hair.

When your boots want re-soling and heeling,
And your shirts are wanting a mend;
Your toothbrush is black and mouldy
Since you used it to spread Soldier's Friend.

'Tis then that the words 'Kit inspection'
Bring fear to the hearts of the brave,
And you start to tremble with wind up
Till you can't hold a razor to shave.

You start going round on the borrow
To your mates in another platoon.
In the canteen that night at supper
You knock off a knife, fork and spoon.

That night you lie on your bed thinking
Till weary you fall off to sleep
With some well thought out plan you've invented
Which you from ill favour may keep.

Then you stand by your bed like a hero
Without any socks to your feet,
And you swear to yourself that next pay day
You'll make up your small kit complete.

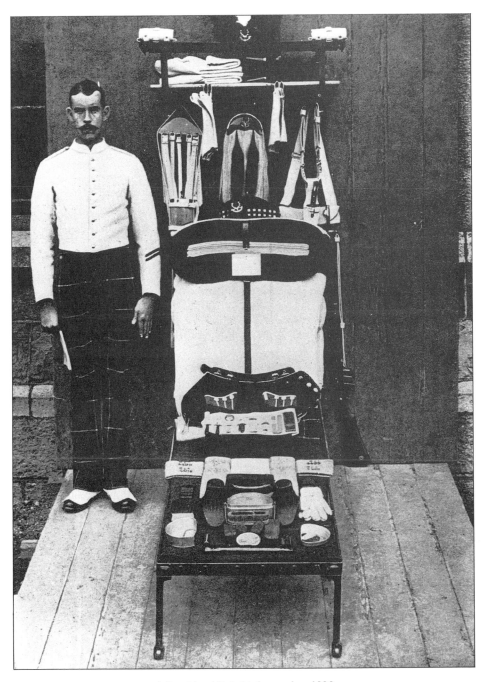

A Scottish soldier's kit layout, late 1890s

lthough conscription was in force in Britain from 1916 to 1918 and from 1939 to 1963 it seems to have produced little in song by way of direct comment on the lot of the pressed man, other than 'Kitchener's Army'* and its Second World War adaptation, 'Belisha's Army'.* Much reliance has been placed on volunteers, and songs like 'The Warwickshire RHA'* must have led many a man to enlist. On the other hand, there are many warnings of the hardships and dangers of army life, and even what one might call anti-recruiting songs.

Both conscripts and volunteers were quick to complain at least in song about the conditions they found on joining. Camp life, drill, food, pay, spit and polish, military discipline: all these combined with a Kafkaesque sense of lost identity to induce a bleak outlook, relieved only by natural resilience and humour. Despite all this, the army succeeded in instilling a new feeling of belonging, an identity cast in its own mould. New habits of thought and behaviour were inculcated. *Esprit de corps* was fostered by information on history and traditions, and the preaching of superiority. During my national service in the mid-1950s I was in the cavalry, which was unquestionably superior to the infantry, which was in turn more than a cut above, say, the RASC. Almost everyone looked down on the pay corps, the catering corps, and the pioneer corps. These could always despise civilians. The British Army as a whole was superior to all other armies, just as the British at large were superior to all foreigners.

Inter-regimental rivalries, sometimes stretching back for centuries, could lead to fights when particularly antagonistic elements happened to meet. Songs vaunted the virtues, often sexual, of particular regiments.

Servicewomen seem to have sung as much as the men, and on similar occasions. Much of the repertoire, bawdy material included, seems to have been common to both sexes. The ATS, WAAFs and army nurses had their own unofficial anthems, but appear to have developed little else peculiar to their own circumstances. Perhaps more remains to be discovered.

· *JOIN THE BRITISH* · ARMY

This song of Irish origin has circulated both inside and outside the army since Victorian times. One version refers to 'Ta-ra-ra-boom-deray' (popularised in 1891) and its singer: 'Lottie Collins got no drawers. Will you kindly lend her yours? For she's got to go away To sing ta-ra-ra-boom-deray.' An alternative has: 'Kilted soldiers have no drawers. Won't you kindly lend them yours? For the poor should help the poor And join the British Army.' Singers would insert at appropriate points the names of NCOs they disliked.

When I was young I used to be
As fine a man as you could see.
The Prince of Wales he said to me,
'Come and join the British Army'.
Toora loora loora loo,
They're looking for monkeys up in the zoo.
If I had a face like you
I'd join the British Army.

Sarah Conlon baked a cake,
She said for poor old Slattery's sake.
Sure, I threw myself into the lake,
Pretending I was barmy.
Toora loora loora loo,
I've made my mind up what to do:
I'll work me ticket home to you,
And leave the British Army.

Sergeant Snooks he went away.
His wife got in the family way,
And the only words that she could say
Were, 'Blame the British Army'.
Toora loora loora loo,
Me curse upon the motley crew
Who took me [your] darling boy from me [you]
To join the British Army.

Corporal Smith's a terrible lout:
Just give him a couple of jars of stout
And he'll rout the enemy with his mouth,
And save the British Army.
Toora loora loora loo,
I've made my mind up what to do:
I'll work me ticket home to you,
And leave the British Army.

Volunteers of the Kingsbridge 5th Hay Tor Battalion, North Devon Regiment, on Salisbury Plain, c. 1902

· THE WARWICKSHIRE · RHA

Martial songs have a long history of inspiring men to join up. John J. Blockley's 'The Scarlet and the Blue', written in the 1870s, seems to have been intended to attract farm workers to the colours. It was popularised on both sides of the Atlantic by the Irish comedians, Ed Harrigan and Tony Hart, and soldiers sang it to keep their spirits up during the Boer and First World Wars.

One variant features the Royal Artillery, another the Royal Horse Artillery, and a third, the Warwickshire RHA. In the version given here the chorus has been influenced by the words of 'We Are Fred Karno's Army' (for which, see page 33). Blockley's original text runs: 'Hurrah for the scarlet and the blue, And the helmets a-glittering in the sun. The bay'nets flash like lightning to the beating of the old bass drum. Hurrah for dear old England and her flag that's waving in the sky. When the captain of the reg'ment says, "We'll conquer or we'll die".'

A further adaptation, made in 1916, changed a number of details and invited volunteers to join the IRA. This was sung by both British and Irish members of the International Brigade in Spain during the Civil War, and Harold Wirdnam (see Introduction) learned it in India in the 1930s.

I was a jolly ploughboy, ploughing in the fields one day,
When a silly thought came into my mind, I thought I'd run away.
I was tired of the dear old country and the place where I was born,
So I've been and joined the army and I'm off tomorrow morn.
(*Chorus*)
Hurrah for the RHA. See the spurs as they glitter in the sun,
And the horses gallop like lightning with a fifteen-pounder gun;
And when we get to France, my boys, the Kaiser he will say:
'Hoch, hoch, mein Gott, what a jolly fine lot are the Warwickshire RHA.'

I lay aside my old grey mare, I lay aside my plough,
I lay aside my four-tined fork; I shall not want them now.
No more will I go harvesting or reap the golden corn,
For I've been and joined the army and I'm off tomorrow morn.

Just one thing I must leave behind, and that's my Nelly dear.
I've promised I'd be true to her if I were far or near.
So if ever I return again I'll let you all see me,
For I'm going to do the churchyard walk, and a captain's wife she'll be.

Barrack room of the 1890s

*King's Birthday Parade on the Maidan,
Bangalore, India, 1938*

ᴄᵋᴦ · *BUNGAY ROGER* · ᴐᴔᴏ

The ordinary man's bewilderment and resentment at his first contact with the rules and routines of the army are perennial subjects for song. At the time of the Napoleonic Wars in a street ballad entitled 'The Awkward Recruit' the eponymous soldier complains of the difficulty of the drill, the itchiness of his flour-anointed queue, and the tightness of his stock. The song remained current with soldiers at least until the First World War, with the emphasis on drill and diet. Under titles as diverse as 'Bungay Town', 'Muddley Barracks', 'The Yorkshire Blinder' and 'The Gloucester Blinder' it can still be heard from the occasional country singer.

Tune: 'Sheepskin and Beeswax'

> Oh I be come from Bungay town, they call I Bungay Roger.
> They asked I o'er and o'er again if I would be a soldier.
> They asked I o'er and o'er again if I would earn a shillin'.
> Cor, blast, says I, I'll have a try just to show I'm willin'.
> *(Chorus)*
> *With a fol on a day, fol on a day, fol on a day till I get home.*
>
> They marched I round the barrack square a-doing my duty manual.
> They marched I round the barrack square a-doing my duty in general.
> 'Eyes right. Eyes left. Cor, blast yer, hold yer head up,'
> And afore I'd answered half a bloody word they bugger I in the lock-up.
>
> They marched I to the dinin' hall as hungry as a hunter,
> But we daren't touch a goddamn bit till the officer had been round, sir.
> Up jumped the orderly sergeant: 'Any complaints today, sir?'
> Well, up jumped I: 'Two dirty great spuds and a lump of fat, cor blast yer what
>   a mouthful.'
>
> I wish I wor back on the farm pushin' a bloody ol' plough, sir.
> I wish I wor back on the farm milkin' a bloody ol' cow, sir.
> I wish I wor back on the farm toppin', tailin' turnips
> With a dirty ol' knife and a rusty ol' fork, cor blast yer, how I'd cut 'em.

ℰ · COME ON AND JOIN · ℰ

Lord Kitchener was made Secretary of State for War on the outbreak of hostilities in 1914. He set about recruiting and training large numbers of men into what came to be known as 'Kitchener's armies'. Most of these volunteers met their deaths during the Battle of the Somme in 1916. Australian soldiers had their own version of the song, mentioning William Hughes, who became their Prime Minister in 1915. The British minister who introduced conscription in 1939 was Leslie Hore Belisha, and inevitably he was commemorated, too.

Tune: 'I wanna be back home in Dixie'

A.
Come on and join, come on and join,
Come on and join Lord Kitchener's army.
Ten bob a week, plenty grub to eat,
Bloody great boots make blisters on yer feet.

B.
Why don't you join, why don't you join,
Why don't you join Billy Hughes's army?
Six bob a day and nothing to eat,
Great big boots and blisters on your feet,
Why don't you join, why don't you join,
Why don't you join Billy Hughes's army?

C.
We had to join up, we had to join up,
We had to join Belisha's army.
Sitting on the grass, polishing the brass;
Bloody great spiders crawling up your arse.
We had to join up, we had to join up,
We had to join Belisha's army.
If it wasn't for the war we'd have fucked off long before,
Hore Belisha, you're barmy.

Volunteers taking the oath in a recruiting office at the White City, London, 1915

• *WHY DID WE JOIN* •
THE ARMY?

Soldiers sang this self-derisively from the First World War until at least the 1950s. The last words were more normally 'fucking well barmy'. An air force version of 1940 begins: 'Why did I join the RAF? Why can't I learn to fly?' The tune was one of the official marches of the King's Liverpool Regiment.

Tune: 'Here's to the Maiden of Bashful Fifteen'

> Why did we join the army, boys?
> Why did we join the army?
> Why did we come to Salisbury Plain?
> We must have been ruddy well barmy.

· I DON'T WANT TO · JOIN THE ARMY

A song from *The Passing Show of 1914*, a revue at the London Hippodrome, was seized on and parodied by soldiers of the First World War. Their version was heard again in France in 1939, sung by members of the new British Expeditionary Force. Canadian soldiers also sang it. An air force version of 1916 is quoted in Terence Rattigan's play, *Flare Path* (1942).

Tune: 'On Sunday I walk out with a soldier'

> I don't want to join the army, I don't want to go to war;
> I'd rather hang around Piccadilly underground,
> And live off the earnings of a high-born lady.
> I don't want a bullet up me arsehole,
> I don't want me ballocks shot away;
> I'd rather stay in England, in merry, merry England,
> And fornicate me bleeding life away.

Postcard of the First World War, showing a spartan RAMC barracks

᎒ · WE ARE IN · ᎒ KITCHENER'S ARMY/ WE ARE FRED KARNO'S ARMY

Despite its gloomy tune and self-deprecatory words, this was a favourite marching song for half a century. All three services had versions. In the First World War there were King George's Army, Kitchener's Army and Fred Karno's Army, Navy or Air Corps (Karno being a comedian who specialised in the portrayal of gross incompetence). The ASC (Army Catering Service, otherwise known as Ally Sloper's Cavalry – Sloper being the blundering hero of a comic strip) was varied to the RFC (Royal Flying Corps), or, with Australians and New Zealanders, the ANZAC. In the Second World War, Hitler replaced the Kaiser, and the ASC was updated to the RSC (Royal Service Corps, later the RASC). There were both ASR (Air Sea Rescue) and MTB (Motor Torpedo Boat) versions.

Version A here comes from Frank Richards (1883–1961) of the Royal Welch Fusiliers, who, as Robert Graves pointed out – Graves served in the same regiment, and knew him – 'brought off a twenty-thousand-to-one chance' by surviving four years of war in France. Richards published a remarkable book about his experiences, entitled *Old Soldiers Never Die* (1933). A group of old soldiers from Stoke-on-Trent who had been prisoners-of-war together in Italy in the 1940s recorded version B, along with many other songs, in 1971.

Tune: 'The Church's One Foundation'

A.
We are in Kitchener's army, the ragtime ASC.
We cannot fight, we cannot shoot, what bloody use are we?
But when we get to Berlin we'll hear the Kaiser say,
'Hoch, hoch! Mein Gott, what a bloody fine lot to draw six bob* a day.'

B.
We are Fred Karno's army, we are the RSC.
We cannot fight, we cannot fuck, what bleeding good are we?
And when we get to Berlin old Hitler he will say,
'Hoch, hoch, mein Gott, what a fucking fine lot are the boys of the RSC.'

* Some men specially enlisted at the beginning of the war in 1914 were paid six shillings a day.

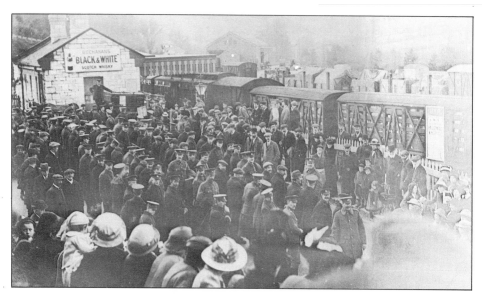

Soldiers of the King's Own Regiment waiting for a troop train at Kingsbridge, Devon, early in the First World War

ᚢ · OUR ESSEX CAMP · ᚢ

The rigours of army camp life are another classic source of soldiers' complaints. A popular song of 1915 by William Jerome and Walter Donaldson was quickly taken up by the troops, and its chorus adapted to words of their own. During the Second World War the parody had a new lease of life under the title of 'Larkhill Camp'.

Tune: 'Down Home in Tennessee'

> Down in our Essex camp,
> That's where we get the cramp
> Through sleeping in the damp;
> We're not allowed a lamp.
> All we get there each day
> Is 'Left, right', all the way;
> Sergeants calling, lance-jacks bawling,
> 'Get out on parade'.
>
> We go to bed at night,
> You ought to see the sight.
> The earwigs on the floors
> All night are forming fours.
> If we're in bed in the morning
> You will hear the sergeant yawning:
> 'Show a leg there, show a leg there',
> Way down in our Essex camp.

⸎ · *ORDERLY SONG* · ⸎

The emphasis moves here from food to those who serve it. The song, by G. E. H. Keesey, was published in 1915. I have a feeling that it was intended for university students at a TA camp where they would have been expected to take a turn as dining room orderlies. The tune comes from *The Scottish Students' Song Book*, and 'swish' (squish: marmalade) was university slang. Other slang words used are 'trog' (prog: food) and 'ackers and tosh' (bread and cheese).

Tune: 'Solomon Levi'

At six o'clock on a shiny morn we start our little day.
We wash the mugs and wipe the jugs and clear the pots away;
We stoke the stoves and butter the loaves and neatly spread the swish,
And tenderly drop a pile of slop in every waiting dish.
(Chorus)
Oh orderly, orderly, oh the orderly day.
Poor sore orderly, tra la la la la la la la la la la.
Six o'clock of a shiny morn we start our little day,
And all day long we're making meals and clearing meals away.
It's: 'Orderly, swish', 'Orderly, tosh', 'Orderly, tea this way'.
Who would be an orderly upon an orderly day?

When breakfast's done we've just begun our weary round of work –
And evil light upon the wight that tries his job to shirk,
A ravening crowd that roars aloud we feed with might and main,
And when they've splashed the plates we've washed we wash them all
    again.

The spotted dog's magnificent trog, and so is Irish stew;
I'm a regular glutton for roasted mutton when I haven't the washing
    to do.
Still, ackers and tosh is easy to wash compared with plates of fat:
I'd rather be fed on cheese and bread than wash for a week of that.

Now just one crumb of chilly comfort has the orderly got,
That when the rest have done their best, why, he can finish the lot.
One cheery ray lights up the day when labour he would spurn,
That when he's laid the scullery maid the others can have their turn.

✺ · BLANDFORD IN THE · ✺ MUD

Relentless drill, exhausting PT, spartan living conditions and the constant threat of punishment all emerge in vivid detail from this anonymous printed sheet of the First World War. No tune is specified, and the piece may have been intended simply as verse. Gordon Hall has put his own tune to it. Joe Driscoll, a friend of his mother's, partly copied the words into a letter home, though the news of his death in the trenches arrived first. After the war the sheet was re-issued under the title of 'Blandford Camp', with a revised last verse:

> Now the war is over and we've whacked old Kaiser Billy,
> To shoot him would be merciful and absolutely silly.
> We'll hook him out of Holland and bring him Blandford way,
> And I'll bet it won't be long before he droops and fades away.

There's an isolated, desolated spot I'd like to mention,
Where all you hear is 'Stand at ease', 'Slope arms', 'Quick march', 'Attention'.
It's miles away from anywhere, by Gad, it is a rum 'un,
A chap lived here for fifty years and never saw a woman.

There are lots of little huts, all dotted here and there;
For those who have to live inside I've offered many a prayer.
Inside the huts there's rats as big as any nanny goat;
Last night a soldier saw one fitting on his overcoat.

For breakfast every morning just like Old Mother Hubbard
You double round the bloomin' hut and jump up at the cupboard.
Sometimes you get bacon and sometimes lively cheese
That forms platoon upon your plate, orders arms and stands at ease.

It's sludge up to the eyebrows, you get it in your ears,
But into it you've got to go without a sign of fear;
And when you've had a bath of sludge you just set to and groom,
And get cleaned up for next parade, or else it's orderly room.

Week in, week out, from morn till night, with full pack and a rifle,
Like Jack and Jill you climb the hills – of course, that's just a trifle.
'Slope arms', 'Fix bayonets', then 'Present', they fairly put you through it,
And as you stagger to your hut the sergeant shouts 'Jump to it'.

There's another kind of drill especially invented for the army,
I think they call it Swedish and it nearly drives you barmy.
This blinking drill it does you good, it makes your bones so tender
You can coil yourself up like a snake and crawl beneath the fender.

With tunics, boots and puttees off you quickly get the habit,
You gallop up and down the hills just like a blooming rabbit.
'Heads backward bend', 'Arms upward stretch', 'Heels raise', then
   'Ranks change places',
And later on they make you put your kneecaps where your face is.

Now when this war is over and we've captured Kaiser Billy,
To shoot him would be merciful and absolutely silly.
Just send him down to Blandford there among the rats and clay,
And I'll bet it won't be long before he droops and fades away.

A postcard home of Aldershot Camp

✵ · THE RIFLE BRIGADE/ · ✵ THE GLOUCESTER BOYS/THE BUFFS

The closer some regiments were, the keener the rivalry. The Rifle Brigade and the King's Royal Rifle Corps were alike in military skill. The Gloucestershire Regiment and the Ox. and Bucks. (Oxford and Buckinghamshire Light Infantry) were geographically close, as were the Royal West and Royal East ('the Buffs') Kent Regiments. Version A was current during the First World War, and probably the others, too, though B was learned in the 1930s. Two shillings and sixpence was the sum payable weekly by the father of an illegitimate child under an affiliation order. The tunes of A and C are the respective regimental marches.

A. *Tune: 'I'm Ninety-five'*
The Rifle Brigade is going away
To leave the girls in the family way.
The KRRs are left behind,
They've two-and-six a week to find.

B.
The Gloucester boys are going away,
They're leaving the girls in the family way.
The Ox. and Bucks. are coming to stay,
And them poor buggers'll have to pay.

C. *Tune: 'The Buffs'*
The Buffs, the Buffs are going away,
Leaving the girls in the family way,
Leaving the Royal West Kents to pay,
Leaving the Royal West Kents to pay.
With a knife, fork, spoon,
A razor, comb and a lather brush,
Knife, fork, spoon,
A razor, comb and a lather brush.

Gloucestershire volunteers leaving for South Africa during the Boer War

ℭ⅁ · WE ARE THE · ℰℒℭ
KENSINGTON BOYS/
FIRST HERTS. BOYS

'Bags of swank' is the phrase with which drill sergeants habitually exhorted men to march, and the song exudes the same sentiment. Variants of its words include 'The Warwickshire Lads' from 1914, 'The Guildford Boys' (Queen's Royal Surrey Regiment) from the 1930s, and no doubt many more. In 1940 children evacuated to Wales sang: 'We are the Brummagem kids'.

Version A here was sung in France and England in the early days of the First World War by members of the Kensington contingent of the Territorial Army. B was learned by 'Nibs' Matthews while serving with the First Battalion, Hertfordshire TA, between 1939 and 1941.

Tune: 'Who were you with last night?'

A.
We are the Kensington Boys, we are the Kensington Boys.
We spend our tanners, we mind our manners,
We are respected wherever we go.
When we're marching down the High Street, Ken.
Doors and windows open wide.
You can hear the sergeant shout,
'Put those blooming Woodbines out'.
We are the Kensington Boys.

Gordon Highlanders on the way to Aberdeen railway station on the first leg of their journey to France, 1939. Some of these men were obliged to surrender at St Valery, and to spend the rest of the war as prisoners

B.
We are the First Herts. Boys, we are the First Herts. Boys.
We know our manners, we spend our tanners,
We are respected wherever we go.
When we're marching down the king's highway,
Doors and windows open wide, wide.
We're the boys that drink brown ale
Out of a pisspot or out of a pail,
We are the First Herts. Boys.

· HERE THEY COME ·

The mixture of boasting and self-deprecation, pride and implied protest, is characteristic of many soldiers' songs. This was sung during the First World War, and probably afterwards, too. The tune is one of the regimental marches of the Royal West Surrey Regiment (formerly the Second Foot).

Tune: part of 'Braganza'

Here they come, here they come,
Silly great buggers every one;
Half-a-crown a week to pay
For putting a girl in the family way.

Here they come, here they come,
Second of Foot but second to none.
Here they come, here they come,
Second of Foot but second to none.

Bullshit, bullshit,
Covered from head to foot in it.
Bullshit, bullshit,
Covered from head to foot in it.

Here they come, the dirty lot,
They chased the girls in Aldershot.
Now they're off to Salisbury Plain
To start their dirty work again.

The 5th (Northumberland) Fusiliers – nicknamed 'The Old and the Bold' – on the march near Swindon, 1897

☙ · I'LL NEVER FORGET · ❧
THE DAY

The late John Gregson learned this song, together with many others, while serving in the Royal Field Artillery in India between 1929 and 1936. It circulated among soldiers at least until the Second World War, with the Royal Artillery mentioned in the second line. There was also a WAAF version, beginning: 'I'll never forget the day I enlisted on the spree To be a little Waafie in the Royal Waafery.'

Tune: based on 'When the roll is called up yonder'

> I'll never forget the day when I enlisted on the spree
> To be a scruffy driver in the field artillery.
> Oh my heart is aching and a-breaking to see civvy life once more.
> Oh you ought to see the drivers on a Friday night
> Polishing up their harness in the candlelight,
> For there's going to be an inspection in the morning
> In the little harness room across the square.
> I'll be there, I'll be there,
> And the battery sergeant-major he'll be there.
> When they're filing out to water
> He'll be kissing the colonel's daughter
> In the little harness room across the square.

ᘓᕽ · *I CANNA SEE THE* · ᕽᘓ
TARGET

Men of the Black Watch sang this during the Second World War on the way to rifle practice at the butts.

Tune: 'The Nut Brown Maiden'

> I canna see the target,
> I canna see the target.
> Och bring the target nearer,
> It's ower far awa'.

ᘓᕽ · *THE WARWICKSHIRE* · ᕽᘓ
YEOMANRY

The emphasis here is on sexual prowess. The crude machismo of such songs can mask a lack of confidence in the singers, or can even hide their innocence. Squadron Leader Bob Godfrey, late of the Canadian Air Force, has a touching story from the Second World War: 'There was . . . the pink-cheeked flight-sergeant who had been singing lustily in the mess about a hippopotamus revelling in the joys of masturbation. On the way home in the damp and dark of the English countryside, he casually asked, "What does masturbation mean?" He wore the Distinguished Flying Medal under his wings.'

Tune: 'The Soldier's Alphabet' or 'If Moonshine Don't Kill Me'

> Oh merry, oh merry, oh merry are we,
> We are the Warwickshire Yeomanry.
> (*Chorus*)
> *Sing high, sing low, wherever we go,*
> *The Warwickshire Yeomanry never say no.*
>
> We can ride, we can fight, we can fuck all the night,
> We are the prostitutes' pride and delight.

George Hall (see Introduction) served with the Royal Sussex Regiment
during the First World War

⟨⟨ · THE · ⟩⟩
QUARTERMASTER
STORES

During my national service in the 1950s those working 'in the stores' were envied for having a cushy job as well as for the opportunity to 'fiddle'. The Quartermaster was responsible for the issue of bedding, clothing, and personal equipment such as haversacks and webbing. Earlier, he also controlled both food and ammunition supplies.

According to some Chelsea Pensioners interviewed by Lewis Winstock, the song has been in circulation since the last decade of the nineteenth century. There seems to be no record of it during the First World War, but it was certainly sung by British and American volunteers, who included First War veterans, during the

Spanish Civil War. An arrangement by Box, Cox and Read became a 'hit' in 1940, and the song was popular with civilians and soldiers alike in the Second World War.

The words readily lend themselves to improvisation, and there are many versions, of which the more outrageous seldom appear in print. The Canadians had a variant chorus alluding to the alleged doctoring of army tea: 'My cock is limp, I cannot fuck, The nitrate it has changed my luck.' Gordon Hall's version (given here) has acquired some verses from a quite different song, 'Here's to the Good Old Beer'. In more innocuous forms, 'The Quartermaster Stores' remains popular. I heard it sung recently in the public bar of a Wiltshire pub.

There was ham, ham, mixed up with the jam,
In the stores, in the stores.
There was ham, ham, mixed up with the jam,
In the quartermaster stores.
(Chorus)
My eyes are dim, I cannot see,
I have not brought my specs with me,
I have not brought my specs with me.

Eggs . . . running round on legs.

Cheese . . . green as garden peas.

Bread . . . heavy as lumps of lead.

Meat . . . soled your boots a treat.

Beer . . . makes you feel so queer.

Port . . . turns a prude into a sport.

Whisky . . . makes you feel so frisky.

Gin . . . that brings a girl to sin.

Brandy . . . makes you feel so randy.

Rats . . . big as bloody cats.

Bugs . . . big as deep-sea tugs.

Mice . . . trying to catch the lice.

Fleas . . . all with housemaid's knees.

Slugs . . . drinking from army mugs.

Phil . . . fiddling the till.

Bob . . . playing with his knob.

Frank . . . having a Midland Bank.

Hall . . . he's only got one ball.

Brown . . . with his knackers hanging down.

(Spoken) My name's Hunt, and I'm going home.

✎ · *ANY COMPLAINTS?* · ✐

A long-standing custom in the British Army is for the orderly officer to walk round the men's canteens at mealtimes and to put the ritual question which provides the title and refrain of this song. Ewan MacColl learnt it in 1940 from a group of soldiers of the King's Liverpool Regiment.

When I joined the army a few weeks ago
I left a good home to come here.
I just couldn't eat any breakfast at all,
My stomach was feeling so queer;
For the sight of those browned ham and eggs on the plate
Filled me with loathing, I fear,
But if I had known then, chum, just what I know now
I'd have eaten enough for a year.
(*Chorus*)
Tell me, boys, have you any complaints?

The very next morning they bunged us some fish,
And, believe me, boys, that fish was cute,
For that so-and-so fish it stood up in the dish
And it gave us the fascist salute.
Well, the fellas turned pale as they rose in their seats,
Some of them more than half dead.
You can take it from me that the war would have stopped
If they'd given it to the Nazis instead.

Every Monday for dinner they give us brown stew,
And on Tuesdays as well for a treat.
We get stew so often, chum, that we thank God
There's only seven days in a week.
For the stew is brown stew and there's jollopy tea –
They've all fancy names for the scoff.
It would be far more honest to say that brown stew
Was stew that was bloody browned off.

⚜ · LONGMOOR · ⚜

The quality of army or NAAFI tea gave rise to frequent comments, and it was widely believed that bromide was added to restrain the troops' sexual drive. The practice of parading both for pay and for prayer is also explored in this Royal Engineers' song of the Second World War. Longmoor Camp is near Liss in Hampshire.

Tune: 'The Mountains of Mourne'

Oh Mary, this Longmoor's a wonderful place,
But the system they have here's a fucking disgrace.
There's lots of bands playing and bugles galore,
And the whole fucking thing is a fucking great bore.

There's plenty of Naafi tea, oh never mind,
It's a brew I'm sure Brooke Bonds never designed.
The flavour I'm sure no one ever could place,
But really it's a mixture of polish and paste.

This Longmoor on Thursdays is lovely to see,
With sappers all lined up in columns of three.
'Tis time when the officers sit in their chairs
And dish out the money as if it was theirs.

When you get to them you hand them your book,
Then all you get from them's a dirty black look.
They give you the cash you've fucking well earned,
And before you get out, in the box it's returned.

They tell us on Sundays it's a day we can rest
But we're out in the morning in best battle-dress.
They tell us as Christians to church we must go,
So we're lined up once more in threes in a row.

They tell us that some day this war's going to end,
And a nice load of cash we'll be able to spend.
Then it's goodbye to the army, goodbye to the tea,
And a soldier's farewell to the old CRE.

· 47 ·

·*I WANNA GO HOME*·

The litany of complaint continues with tea, food and pay. Deductions from soldiers' pay were, and are, made for family allotments, the individual replacement of lost clothing and equipment, and the collective assessment for barrack room damages – the last, very much resented. The song dates from the Second World War. Canadian servicemen had separate versions for the army, the navy and the air force. The tune is from a popular song of the day.

Tune: 'Gee, Ma, I Wanna Go Home'

They say that in the army
The beds are very fine,
But how the hell should they know?
They've never slept in mine.
(*Chorus*)
Gee, ma, I wanna go,
But they won't let me go.
Gee, ma, I wanna go home.

They say that in the army
The food is very fine,
But the bread it tastes like sawdust,
The tea's like iodine.

They say that in the army
The pay is very fine;
They give you forty shillings
And take back thirty-nine.

⊂⧉⊃ · ATS SONG · ⧉⊃

The women's services played a considerable part in an auxiliary role during the Second World War and afterwards. Their members were both derided ('Here comes the crack regiment,' said a witty fellow soldier to me on seeing a marching group of WRACs) and courted by male soldiers. Nevertheless they had their own *esprit de corps*.

Tune: 'Coming Round the Mountains'

> If you want to go to heaven when you die,
> You must wear a khaki bonnet with a tie;
> You must wear a khaki bonnet with ATS upon it,
> If you want to go to heaven when you die.
> (*Chorus*)
> *Singing I will if you will, so will I,*
> *Singing I will if you will, so will I;*
> *Singing I will if you will, I will if you will,*
> *I will if you will, so will I.*

⊂⧉⊃ · WE ARE THE WAAFS · ⧉⊃

During the Second World War, when this song was sung, WAAFs served as clerks, cooks, drivers, parachute packers and spotters.

Tune: 'Bobbing Up and Down Like This'

> We are the WAAFs, all dressed in blue,
> Marching along the parade ground, left, right, one, pause, two.
> We know the RAF don't like us, but very fine girls are we.
> If it wasn't for the girls in the WAAF,
> Where would the airmen be?

ATS women manning a predictor at an anti-aircraft site in Scotland, 1943

· IT WASN'T THE · WAAFS THAT WON THE WAR

Apparently, the song originally ran: 'It wasn't the Wrens that won the war . . . The ATS were there before', and units of the ATS would sing it on the march. Even this nurses' adaptation seems to have left the primacy to the ATS in verse two. Nursing sisters returning to civilian hospitals immediately after the Second World War taught this version to their young colleagues.

Tune: 'Mademoiselle from Armentières'

> It wasn't the WAAFs that won the war, *parlez-vous*,
> It wasn't the WAAFs that won the war, *parlez-vous*.
> It wasn't the WAAFs that won the war:
> The nursing staff were there before.
> (*Chorus*)
> *Inky Pinky parlez-vous.*
>
> The ATS were manning guns . . .
> While the nursing staff were rubbing bums.
>
> It wasn't the Wrens that got the men . . .
> The nursing staff were there again.

· STAND BY YOUR · BEDS

This injunction was a time-honoured military ritual which heralded the hated ceremony of kit inspection, when men stood to attention by their beds while inspecting officers scrutinised their bedding and clothing, laid out in prescribed patterns. Studs in best boots were polished, spare leather laces curled into neat whorls and tied with black cotton, haversacks squared off with cardboard or even plywood, Brasso tins were scraped clean of paint save for the circle with the name, and so on.

A variant for the last two lines was: 'He should have his rings Stuffed up his fucking arsehole.' Although the song refers with some acerbity to an air force officer it was sung by army national servicemen in the 1950s.

Tune: a fanfare

> Stand by your beds,
> Here comes the air vice-marshal.
> He's got four rings
> But he's only got one arsehole.

⊂⊛ · STAND ON THE · ⊛⊃ SQUARE

Brilliantly polished boots, carefully pressed uniforms and spotlessly blancoed webbing came very high on the list of military virtues. This epigrammatic song was learned by an RASC national serviceman at Aldershot in 1951. He had a variant for line two: 'Here comes the adjutant with a bloody great erection.'

> Stand on the square, boys, ready for an inspection.
> Here comes the adjutant, heading in our direction.
> Boots highly polished, but somebody's pinched me blanco.
> You've got to admit your kit is in shit,
> But ain't life grand?

· CHAPTER TWO ·

PUNISHMENT

DEFAULTERS

The shades of night are falling fast
When on the air a bugle blast.
I start to run, I start to swear,
I dash across the barrack square: Defaulters.

My brow is sad, I long for sleep,
Between the sheets I fain would creep.
My days of peace and rest are past,
For all day long I hear that blast: Defaulters.

In barrack rooms I see the light
Of cigarettes all burning bright.
I get no time to smoke at all,
For still I hear the bugle call: Defaulters.

The old hand says, 'Be careful there.
Beware the stony barrack square,
Lest you should stumble, chance to fall,
And fail to heed the bugle call: Defaulters.'

A soldier cries, 'Give me a light',
And tries to stop my headlong flight.
I almost barge him through the wall,
For louder yet there sounds the call: Defaulters.

Life full of misery and woe;
Out of the lines I cannot go.
I'd love to choke the bugler tall
Who rends the air with strident call: Defaulters.

I'd kill [him] if I had my way;
Lifeless, unbeautiful he'd lay;
But even so some other loon
Would play that pestilential tune: Defaulters.

One aspect of service life that at best inspired anxiety and fear and at worst aroused resentment and even rebellion was the draconian disciplinary system. Even trivial offences – a button left undone, a spot of metal polish allowed to dry on a buckle, a bootlace incorrectly displayed for kit inspection – could result in a soldier's being placed on a charge, and I am speaking not of the remote past but from my own experiences. If a precise clause in the military code did not serve, there was always the all-embracing charge of 'conduct to the prejudice of good order and military discipline'.

An offender (called a 'defaulter'), with cap off in sign of disgrace, was marched in front of his battalion or squadron OC, usually a major, and required to answer the charge while standing rigidly to attention. A common punishment was CB – confined to barracks. George Coppard's description from the First World War (his crime was 'dumb insolence' – glaring at an NCO) would be instantly familiar to generations of servicemen:

> 'Jankers' was the common name for CB, and from the moment of sentence I became liable to the whims and dictates of the police sergeant. Starting at two or three minutes after reveille and such other awkward times as could be conceived, the bugler would blast out a call which, translated into words, went: 'You can be a defaulter as long as you like, as long as you answer your name.' With other defaulters I had to run at the double to the police tent, answer my name and get told off to my fatigue. The Lord help me if I was late. It was an offence to be late, and usually meant another dose of Jankers. Emptying the urinal tubs was always the first job; you could bank on it. Other fatigues, such as peeling spuds, washing thousands of plates and doing cookhouse chores, succeeded each other with monotonous regularity throughout the day . . . I like to think I enjoyed Jankers, for it gave me the excuse to grouse, a soldier's traditional privilege. In a sense it was an important part of my army training learning how to be fly and cunning.[56]

For more serious offences a soldier would be remanded to appear before the CO of the regiment, who could award up to twenty-eight days' detention in the guardroom, which was administered by the (usually hated and feared) provost sergeant and his regimental police. Even more heinous crimes – serious theft, desertion, mutiny – were dealt with by courts martial. Corporal Jim Daly, executed in India for mutiny in 1920, was the last man in the British Army to suffer death for a military offence.

All these matters are reflected in songs, which are variously light-hearted, sentimental, defiant or deeply moving.

Ꮆ · McCAFFERY · ᎷᏬ

Patrick M'Caffrey (the name is spelt in many different ways) was born in Ireland, near Mullingar. His family later moved to Carlow, where his father was the governor of a lunatic asylum. His mother died, and his father left for America, where he seems to have disappeared. Patrick moved to Mossley, near Stalybridge in Lancashire, to join the household of a Mrs Murphy, who had wet-nursed him as a baby. After working for a time in cotton mills he enlisted in the army, inflating his age by at least a year to reach the statutory eighteen. In October 1860 he reported to Fulwood Barracks at Preston to receive training before joining his chosen regiment, the 32nd (Cornwall Light Infantry).

On Friday, 13 September 1861 M'Caffrey was acting as picket-sentry near the officers' quarters. The adjutant, Captain Hanham, came out to complain of the noise made by some children who were playing. He ordered M'Caffrey to send them away, but first to take their parents' names. When he judged M'Caffrey's compliance to be half-hearted, he sent him to the guardroom. Next day, the CO, Colonel Crofton, sentenced him to fourteen days' CB for neglect of duty.

M'Caffrey seems to have gone quietly afterwards to his barrack room, taken his rifle, and coolly fired at Hanham as he was crossing the square with Crofton. Both officers were mortally wounded with the same shot.

M'Caffrey was tried at Liverpool Assizes in December 1861, and found guilty of wilful murder. He was hanged outside Kirkdale (now Walton) Jail on 11 January 1862 before a sympathetic crowd of some thirty to forty thousand people.

The song (with the victim's name assuming various forms) seems to have circulated without being printed for the best part of a century. My father heard it in the Leicestershire Regiment in the 1920s. Tom Langley, who served in the Grenadier Guards from 1924 to 1927 'heard it sung quietly, many times, by . . . old soldiers', though not by 'the canteen king', who 'believed it was against the King's Rules and Regulations and the Standing Orders of the Brigade of Guards to sing it'. J. Imray heard it in 1934 from his brother, who was in the 4th Battalion, Northumberland Fusiliers, TA. When he joined the Duke of Wellington's Regiment at Halifax later in the same year he was told:

> We were now Conservatives, i.e. loyal to the government of the day. We were not allowed to sing two songs, 'Home Sweet Home' and 'The Red Flag'. Thirdly, we were not allowed to wear black shirts. That was the dream of the Blackshirt Party, [led by] Oswald Mosley.

'McCaffery' was not mentioned, but when Cyril Nuttall joined the 47th (Lancashire) Regiment at Fulwood Barracks (the scene of the original incident) in 1938 he heard it sung by an Irish soldier and was told that it was forbidden. At about the same time in India, according to John Gregson, if anyone sang 'McCaffery' in the canteen a man was posted at the door to see that no NCO or orderly officer was in the vicinity. Prisoners-of-war sang it in Germany during the 1940s. Roy Harris learned it as late as 1951 while serving in the Royal Artillery. Gordon Hall sang it during his national service, also with the artillery, in the Middle East. The circumstances were intriguing. He was serving a sentence of twenty-one days in the regimental guardroom, and while taking a shower sang it so loudly that it could be heard all over the camp. Shortly afterwards the regiment was paraded for a 'pep talk' to counteract the subversive influence the song was felt to exert.

The version given here comes from the manuscript book of songs, poems and jokes compiled in India in 1937 by William Blackmore, a clerk in the 1st Devonshire Regiment.

Tune: 'The Croppy Boy'

Now young men take warning from my sad tale
As here I lay in Kirkdale Jail.
My thoughts and feelings no one can tell
As I lay here in my condemned cell.

I was scarcely eighteen years of age
When into the army I did engage.
I left my factory with a good intent
To join the forty-second regiment.

To Fortwell [Fulwood] Barracks I then did go
To serve some time in that depot.
From trouble and blame I was never free,
Then my captain took a dislike to me.

When stationed there on guard one day,
Some soldiers' children came out to play.
From the officers' quarters my captain came,
And bid me take their parents' names.

My officer's orders I did not fulfil,
But solemnly against my will
I took one name instead of three:
Neglect of duty he then charged me.

At the Orderly Room I did appear.
My CO refused my sad tale to hear.
My sentence then was quickly signed:
To Fortwell Barracks I was confined.

When to my duty I did go
With heavy burden my heart did grow;
With loaded rifle I did appear
To shoot my captain on the barrack square.

With loaded rifle and careful aim –
Across the square my captain came –
It was my captain I meant to kill,
But I shot my colonel against my will.

I had no mother to break her heart;
I had no father to take my part,
But I had one friend, a girl was she,
Who would lay down her life to save McCaffery.

It was at Liverpool Assizes my trial was heard:
I did the deed and shed the blood.
The judge he said to me, 'McCaffery,
Prepare yourself for the gallows tree.'

Now it was in England this young man died,
But it was in Ireland that his body lies;
And every soldier that passes that way
Says, 'Lord have mercy on McCaffery.'

All young officers take warning from me,
Treat all your men with decency.
For it was nothing else but perjury
That caused the death of McCaffery.

· THE REPRIEVE ·

The theme of a soldier saved from execution by a last-minute pardon has a long history. Dispensers of clemency, at least in song, have included the Duke of York (him of the ten thousand men), General Wolfe, King George and Prince Albert. Although he served in the Grenadier Guards, Tom Langley (1907–80) had this 'real old soldiers' song' from his aunt, who was born in 1873. He was unsure of its 'nice mournful tune', but thought it resembled that of 'The Daring Young Man on the Flying Trapeze'.

Wild blew the gale in Gibraltar one night
As a soldier lay stretched in his cell,
And anon, 'mid the darkness, the moon's silver light
On his countenance dreamily fell.
Naught could it reveal but a man true as steel
That oft for his country had bled,
And the glance of his eye might a grim king defy,
For despair, fear and trembling had fled.

In rage he had struck a well-merited blow
At a tyrant who held him in scorn,
And his fate at a drum-head court-martial was sealed:
Honest Joe was to die in the morn.
Oh, sad was the thought to a man that had fought
'Mid the ranks of the gallant and brave,
To be shot through the breast at a coward's behest,
And laid in a criminal's grave.

The night call had sounded when Joe was aroused
By a step at the door of his cell.
'Twas a comrade with whom he had often caroused
Who came now to bid him farewell.
'Oh, Tom, is it you, come to bid me adieu?
My comrade, let me take your hand.
Now, Tom, don't get wild, or you'll make me a child.
I'm bound for a happier land.'

With hands clasped, in silence Tom mournfully said:
'Have you a request, Joe, to make?
Remember, by me you'll be fully obeyed.
I'll do all I can for your sake.'
'When it's over, tomorrow,' said Joe, filled with sorrow,
'Take this to the lass whom I've sworn
All my fond love to share.' 'Twas a lock of his hair
And a prayer book all faded and worn.

'Here's this watch for my mother, and when you write home,'
And he dashed a bright tear from his eye,
'Say I died with my heart in old Devonshire, Tom,
Like a man and a soldier. Goodbye.'
Then the sergeant on guard at the grating appeared,
And Tom had to leave the cold cell.
By the moon's waning light he called out: 'Goodnight.
God bless you, my comrade. Farewell.'

Grey dawned the morn in a dull cloudy sky.
The blast of the bugle rang clear,
And Joe in his escort went forward to die,
A soldier who did not know fear;
And onward they marched to the dread field of doom.
The tyrant looked down to the ground;
The regiment in line watched with sadness and gloom
While Joe smiled and calmly looked round.
Then soft on the air rose the accents of prayer,
And faint tolled the solemn death bell.
Joe knelt on the sand and with uplifted hand
He murmured a sacred farewell.

'Make ready', exclaimed an imperious voice.
'Present!' struck a chill on each mind.
E'er the last word was spoke there was cause to rejoice:
'Hold, hold', cried a voice from behind.
Then wild were they all as a mounted hussar
Drew rein and cried: 'Mercy. Forbear.'
'It's a pardon, hurrah! A free pardon, hurrah,'
And the muskets rang loud in the air.

Some comrades were locked in each other's embrace;
No more stood the brave soldier dumb.
With loud shout they wheeled to the right about face,
And away to the sound of the drum.
A brighter day dawned in sweet Devon's fair land
When the lovers met, never to part.
He gave her a token, true, warm and unbroken,
The gift of his own gallant heart.

·ONCE TO THE LINE·

Flogging in the British Army was abolished in 1881. Before then its existence was used as an argument by those trying to persuade men not to join. 'The Young Recruit; or, Thirteen Pence a Day', a street ballad printed in the mid-nineteenth century, issued an ironic invitation:

> Come and be a soldier, lads, come, lads come.
> Hark, don't you hear the fife and the drum?
> Come to the battlefield, march, march away;
> Come and lose your eyes and limbs for thirteen pence a day.
>
> Remember we are soldiers, the bravest of the brave;
> Come and be a soldier, then you'll be a slave.
> Come to Colonel White, my lads, but don't pretend to cry,
> For if you are not happy we can flog you till you die.

'Once to the Line' seems to be a descendant of this piece, with 'thirteen pence' adapted to 'eight annas' to fit service in India. The singer, Bill House, learnt it during the First World War from soldiers billeted in his village of Beaminster, Dorset. He suggests that 'when all folks are the garge' (verse one) means 'when people are running about and making a din'.

> Once to the line, to the line I did belong,
> I oftimes saw a pretty face and oftimes sung a song,
> But when I get my liberty and gain my free discharge
> No more will I join the militia, boy, when all folks are the garge.
> (*Chorus*)
> *With your right shoulder forward, quickly march away,*
> *Come and lose your eyes and limbs for eight annas a day.*
>
> The colonel and the adjutant, the biggest old sods of all,
> If you give them any slack jaw to the guardroom you shall go.
> They'll claim you for mutiny or fighting in the room,
> Saying, 'Come in you corporal, do your duty, walk it in to him.'
>
> Early next day morning they'll form you in a square;
> If you give them any slack jaw triangles will be there.
> They'll claim you for mutiny or fighting in the room,
> Saying, 'Come in you corporal, do your duty, walk it in to him.'

ᘓᕉ · YES, AND WE CAN · ᕉᘗ DO IT

Breaking out of the barracks here means quitting them without proper leave. In the days of enclosed camps, this meant climbing a wall or fence to avoid the regimental policeman or guard posted at the gate. The commanding officer of a regiment can still award a soldier up to twenty-eight days' detention in the guardroom (or could in my day), though not the 'pack-drill, bread and water' of the First World War and afterwards. The expression, 'No names, no pack-drill', is a relic of that era.

Tune: 'Early in the Morning'

> Breaking out of barracks. (*ter*)
> (*Chorus*)
> *As you have done before.*
> Parading all unbuttoned.
> Take his name and number.
> Up before the CO.
> Fourteen days' detention.
> Pack-drill, bread and water.
> Yes, and we can do it.

· KEVIN BARRY ·

Kevin Barry was hanged in Dublin on 1 November 1920 for his part in the attack on an army bread lorry, which led to the death of a soldier. It must seem surprising that an Irishman rebelling against British rule in general and the Black and Tans in particular should be sympathetically remembered by British soldiers, but this was indeed the case. Not only did many Irishmen serve in the British Army, but often their songs were adopted by their English, Welsh and Scots comrades. John Gregson learned 'Kevin Barry' while serving in India in the 1930s; Gordon Hall heard it in the NAAFI at a camp near Ismailia in Egypt during the 1950s.

Tune: 'Rolling Home'

On that fatal Monday morning high upon the gallows tree
Kevin Barry gave his young life for the cause of liberty.

Just a lad of eighteen summers but there's no one can deny
As he walked to death that morning he nobly held his head on high.

'Barry, Barry, do not leave us; on the scaffold do not die,'
Cried his broken-hearted mother as she waved her son goodbye.

Barry turned his head in anguish, crying, 'Mother, do not weep.
What I did, I did for Ireland and the cause of liberty.'

Just behind that little bakery where we fought them hand to hand
British soldiers tortured Barry just because he wouldn't tell

All the names of his companions and other things they wished to know.
'Tell them over, and we'll free you,' but Barry proudly answered, 'No.'

'Shoot me like an Irish soldier, do not hang me like a dog.
What I did I did for Ireland and the cause of liberty.'

Another martyr for old Ireland, another murder for the crown,
But with all their brutal courage they couldn't crush the Irish down.

Men like Barry are no cowards, from their foes they do not flee,
But they fight to free old Ireland from the laws of tyranny.

Jim Daly, who was executed for mutiny in 1920. He is wearing the khaki drill uniform of the British soldier in India between the wars

 · *LAY HIM AWAY O'ER* · *THE HILLSIDE*

By coincidence, on 2 November 1920, the day after Kevin Barry's hanging in Dublin, Private James Joseph ('Jim') Daly of the 1st Battalion, Connaught Rangers, was executed by firing squad at Dagshai Prison in the Punjab. He has the distinction of being the last British soldier to suffer death for a military offence: he was convicted of mutiny for leading a refusal of duty as a protest against the atrocities committed in Ireland by the Black and Tans. Sixty-one men of the Connaught Rangers were convicted by courts martial. Of these, fourteen were sentenced to death, and the rest to various terms of imprisonment. All the capital sentences were commuted to life imprisonment except for that on Daly, an ardent republican. Those still in prison in 1922 were released under an amnesty negotiated by the newly established Irish Free State.

Despite an attempted ban, the song circulated in the British Army. On one occasion in India John Gregson was caught singing it while he groomed his horse. The sergeant came up and said:

'More grooming and less singing, Gregson, or your feet won't touch' – which meant I'd be right inside [the guardroom, under arrest]. He wasn't grabbing me for singing. If I'd been singing anything else I'd have got away with it.

The grey dawn had crept o'er the stillness of morning.
The dew-drops they glistened like icicled breath.
The notes of the bugle had sounded its warning:
A young Connaught Ranger lay sentenced to death.
No cold-blooded murder had stained his pure conscience:
He called as a witness his maker on high.
He'd simply been fighting for Ireland's loved freedom;
Arrested and tried, he was sentenced to die.

(*Chorus*)
Lay him away o'er the hillside, along with the brave and the bold.
Inscribe his name on the scroll of fame in letters of purest gold.
'My conscience would never convict me,' he said with his dying breath;
'May God bless the cause of freedom, for which I am sentenced to death.'

He thought of the love of his feeble old mother,
He thought of the colleen so dear to his heart;
The sobs of affection he scarcely could smother,
Well knowing how soon from them both he must part.
He feared not to die, though his heart was near broken,
'Twas simply remembrance of those he loved well;
His rosary he pressed to his heart as a token,
The prayer cheered his heart in a felon's lone cell.

To the grim barrack square the doomed hero was hurried
In the grey of the dawn, ere the sun rose on high;
With head held erect, undaunted, unworried,
The gallant young soldier went proudly to die.
'I blame not my comrades for doing their duty.
Aim straight at the heart,' were the last words he said,
Exposing his breast to the point of the rifle.
The smoke cleared away, the young soldier lay dead.

· THE RAMBLING · ROYAL

Desertion must have crossed every soldier's mind at one time or another, and it frequently features in songs. This one, from the Royal Marines, probably dates from the 1930s. It is clearly based on an Irish rebel ballad of 1798, beginning 'I am a real republican, John Wilson is my name' or 'I am a bold shoemaker, from Belfast town I came'. The hero in the latter version is called Irving. He enlists 'in the train', and his grieving sweetheart offers to help him desert by dressing him 'in her own clothes, that I might go to and fro'. Spurning this classic subterfuge, he deserts unaided, though he is successful only at the second attempt. He then joins the rebel force led by Father Michael Murphy, and fights in 'many a battle', including that at New Ross. The ballad concludes with his challenge to Orangemen.

Oh I am a rambling Royal, from Liverpool I came,
And to my sad misfortune I enlisted in the marines.
Being drunk when I enlisted, not knowing what I'd done,
Until my sober senses returned to me again.

Well I had a girl in Birkenhead, and a true friend, as it seems;
It broke her heart and made her smart to see me in the marines.
She said: 'If you desert, young man, as I do hope you may,
I'll have you in my own bedroom, if you should chance to stay.'

It was at the Chatham depot the officer gave command
That me and two of my comrades that night on guard should stand.
The night being dark and wet and cold, with me did not agree,
So I knocked out a guardroom corporal and ran for my liberty.

Oh I rambled all that livelong night until I lost my way,
And I landed in some farmer's barn and stretched out on the hay;
But when I awoke it was no joke for there all at my head
The sergeant and the officer and two bloody swaddies stood.

Well we had a terrible fight, and I damn near beat them all;
I made my cowardly comrades in agony to bawl,
But they locked me in the glasshouse my sorrows to deplore,
With a man at every window and another at every door.

Well it was early the very next morning I paced the guardhouse round;
I jumped out of a window and felled three of them to the ground;
But the provost and his bullies they was quickly after me,
But I made my way to Birkenhead and so gained my liberty.

Oh I am a rambling Royal, James Cronin is my name.
I can fight as many officers as you'll find in the marines.
I can fight as many Orangemen as ever banged a drum,
And I'll make 'em run before me like a bullet from a gun.

· LEOPOLD JAIL ·

Gordon Hall heard his brother sing this in 1945. His brother in turn had learned the song from a North American Indian in either the Canadian or US Army. The jail in question was used at the time for military prisoners. Leopoldsburg in eastern Belgium may be the place intended.

Tune: 'Down in the Valley'

> Leopold jailhouse, Leopold Jail,
> Serving my sentence in Leopold Jail.
> Six years' hard labour, six years in jail,
> Serving my sentence in Leopold Jail.

Write me a letter, send it by mail,
Please you'll address it to Leopold Jail.
Leopold jailhouse, Leopold Jail,
Serving my sentence in Leopold Jail.

If you don't love me, please let me know,
If you don't love me, please let me know.
Leopold jailhouse, *etc.*

Six years' hard labour, six years in jail,
Serving my sentence in Leopold Jail.
Leopold jailhouse, *etc.*

When you write this letter I'll read every line,
Just answer my question, 'Will you be mine?'
Roses are red, love, violets are blue.
Angels in heaven know I love you.

Know I love you, love, know I love you,
Angels in heaven know I love you.
Leopold jailhouse, *etc.*

· CHAPTER THREE ·

PRISONERS-OF-WAR

TO A DEAD TOMMY

I saw a photo in the enemy press,
Which showed your corpse in battledress,
Comrade, who by fate was chosen
To end his service in death's grip frozen.
Saw no signs of identity;
Remains a mystery.
At home they'll hear the news
Of the sacrifice you didn't refuse.
We prisoners in this hostile land
Would like to shake you by the hand.
Our sacrifice wasn't so great:
Yours was the sternest, hardest, mate.

A funeral in Stalag VIIIB, Germany, 1940s

Soldiers taken prisoner by the enemy share the repertoire of their comrades who continue to fight, save, of course, for any new songs arising after that time for either group. Very little seems to have been written about the experiences of British soldiers held by the Germans during the First World War, but the poet, F. W. Harvey, has testified that he and his officer colleagues sang in their barrack blocks at Gütersloh between evening roll-call and lights out. He mentions 'Drury Lane', and also a song which only he can have introduced, 'The Old Bold Mate', a poem by John Masefield set to music by Ivor Gurney.[57]

During the Second World War British soldiers in German captivity were not allowed to sing 'God Save the King', so they substituted 'Land of Hope and Glory'. The guards had no objection to their learning German songs like the '*Horst Wessel Lied*', but were not pleased when '*wir fahren gegen England*' was altered to '*wir fahren gegen Deutschland*'.

In Italy, prisoners picked up songs – one of which, to the tune of the ubiquitous 'Lili Marlene', begins '*Molto lavorare, poco mangiar*' – from their guards, and also from the peasants whom they worked alongside in the fields. This is how some men from Stoke-on-Trent learned the partisan classic, '*Bella Ciao*'.* They gathered together in 1971, on the initiative of Peter Cheesman of the Victoria Theatre, and their songs and reminiscences of prisoner-of-war life were recorded. Later, a remarkable music-documentary entitled *Hands Up – For You the War is Ended*, was based on this material.

Their repertoire of songs was large, and most of it would have been familiar to many other soldiers. Not so their songs on prison camp life, which provide unique insight. One of these, 'The Prisoner's Lament',* was written by a fellow prisoner of theirs, a Norfolk man called Dick Pavelin. In its quiet way it brilliantly evokes camp life. I very much hope that one of his relatives will see it here. A song from outside the Stoke circle is 'The Kriegie Ballad',* by the Scots poet, Robert Garioch.

Despite the inhuman treatment meted out by the Japanese to prisoners-of-war held in the Far East, British soldiers continued to sing – out of nostalgia, defiance and the will to survive. Their repertoire consisted of any songs, army or civilian, they happened to recall, and also pieces about their experiences by writers among their number who came to the fore. One of these was Harry Berry, an RA gunner-signaller, who wrote songs for concerts held in prisons or camps in Singapore, Taiwan and Tokyo between 1942 and 1944. Another was a Scotsman, Arthur Smith, who wrote 'Down the Mine'* to be sung by his comrades in arms as they marched to work under the eye of the Japanese guards.

· THE KRIEGIE BALLAD ·

The Scots poet, Robert Garioch, was captured at Tobruk in 1942. The song evokes his experiences as a prisoner-of-war at Derna and Benghazi in North Africa, then in Mussolini's Italy at Brindisi, Benevento, Capua and Vetralla. The word which he delicately omits in verse eight is probably 'arseholes'. Eric Newby was also a prisoner in Italy, and his book, *Love and War in the Apennines* (1971), is well worth reading.

Tune: 'Botany Bay'

Yes, this is the place we were took, sir,
And landed right into the bag,
Right outside the town of Tobruk, sir,
So now for some bloody stalag.
(*Chorus*)
Toora lye oora lye addi di,
Toora lye oora lye ay.
Toora lye oora lye addi di,
Here's hoping we're not here to stay.

There was plenty of water in Derna,
But the camp was not very well kept,
For either you slept in the pisshole
Or pissed in the place where you slept.

And when we went on to Benghazi
We had plenty of room, what a treat,
But I wish that the guard was a Nazi –
He might find us something to eat.

We sailed on the good ship *Revalo*;
She carried us over the sea.
You climbed up a forty-foot ladder
Whenever you wanted a pee.

And then we went on to Brindisi
With free melons in fields on the way.
Parades they were quite free and easy
Except that they went on all day.

In transit camp at Benevento
We stayed a long time, truth to tell;
It was there that we all got the shivers
And were all bloody lousy as well.

The sun it grew hotter and hotter;
The shit-trench was streaked red and brown.
The stew it was like maiden's water
With gnats' piss to wash it all down.

With hunger we're nearly demented,
You can see it at once by our looks.
The only ones really contented
Are the greasy fat bastards of cooks.

And then we went on to Capua;
On hard ground we mostly did snooze.
The bedboards got fewer and fewer
And we smashed them up to make brews.

It was there that we got Red Cross parcels
With bully and packets of tea.
Would you swap it for . . .
For want of some brew wood? Not me.

And now it was late in the autumn
And our clothes they were only a farce,
For torn KD shorts with no bottom
Send a helluva draught up your arse.

In Musso's fine box-cars we're riding,
All fitted with wheels that are square.
They park us all night in a siding
But somehow we bloody get there.

At Musso's show camp at Vetralla
They gave us beds, blankets and sheets.
They'd even got chains in the shit-house
But still they had no bloody seats.

We were promised a treat for our Christmas
Of thick pasta-shoota, all hot,
But somehow the cooks got a transfer
And shot out of sight with the lot.

So somewhere they wish us good wishes
That we're not all feeling too queer,
And while they are guzzling our pasta
They wish us a happy New Year.

*Men at Fallingbostel Camp in Germany soon after their liberation
by the 'Desert Rats' (8th Army)*

⟶ · THE PRISONER'S · ⟵
LAMENT

The lot of prisoners held by Germans during the Second World War afterwards inspired many books and films, both fictional and documentary. These tend to concentrate on officers and their escapes. Unlike officers, other ranks were obliged to do hard physical labour, and their living conditions were inferior. The song gives a probably unique insight into the feelings of ordinary prisoners. It was written by a Norfolk man called Dick Pavelin, and learnt from him by a fellow prisoner, Bob Burt of Stoke-on-Trent.

Tune: 'Twenty-one Years in Dartmoor'

The *Posten* says: '*Aufstehen*, and put on your clothes.
You must go to *Arbeit*, as everyone knows;
So fold up your blankets and put them in line:
When I blow the whistle, just get out on time.'
(*Chorus*)
We've counted the days and we've counted the nights.
We've counted the minutes, we've counted the lights.
We've counted the footsteps, we've counted the stars.
We've counted a million of these prison bars.

The prisoners all wake up and shout out: 'Get stuffed.
Of this blinking sleeping we've not had enough.
So down in your flea-pits and stay there till time,
For sixteen hours' *Arbeit* is a very long time.'

Twenty minutes has gone, boys; the first whistle blows.
We all get and scramble and drag on our clothes.
Five minutes to go, chaps; just give it a go:
Don't blow the last whistle, for goodness sake, Joe.

Three and a half years have gone, boys, our spirit's still good.
Sometimes it's all hoeing, or just chopping wood.
They can't get us down, boys, to them it's quite plain:
Just given the time we would do it again.

We've just heard the siren, our spirits soar up:
We hope to see action to liven things up.
But nothing happens, nothing we know;
It just brings back memories of long, long ago.

Oh go back to the *Posten* wtih your payroll
To buy some flea powder for this lousy hole.
It's flies in the daytime, it's fleas all the night;
My poor arms are aching from scratching the bites.

There's just come a letter, our heart's in despair;
Our packets are all robbed, we don't know just where.
Take care of your conserve, you're lost in despair;
You can't keep on working and living on air.

Come on you *Gefangeners* with hearts brave and true,
Don't trust your old *Bauer*, whatever you do.
Don't trust your old *Bauer*, no matter how kind:
You do all his *Arbeit*, and he'll kick your behind.

Group at Stalag VIIIB in Germany. Private Smith of the 2nd Battalion, Lincolnshire Regiment, was a prisoner there from 1940 until 1945

⚶ · *THE GERMAN* · ⚮ CLOCKMAKER

Men separated from their wives for very long periods must have been somewhat ambivalent about songs dealing with cuckoldry. Nevertheless, they seem to have enjoyed the themes both of the chastised and the triumphant seducer. The nationality of the villain of this piece no doubt helped its popularity during the Second World War, especially with those – as in this case – who were prisoners of the Germans. This is not, however, a military song, but one of civilian origin taken by soldiers into the army.

Tune: 'Villikins'

> Now there was a young clockmaker to England once came.
> Benjamin Franks was the young German's name.
> Any clocks to wind up, he would stay all the night,
> And in less than ten minutes he would put their clock right.

(Chorus)
With a toora lye oora lye oora lye ay,
Toora lye oora lye oora lye ay.
Toora lye oora lye oora lye ay,
What for the toora lye ay.

Now this German became all the ladies' delight.
They all went to him to have their clocks put right.
Some went too fast, while others too slow,
But nine out of ten he would make their clocks go.

Now one woman's husband said: 'Wife, Mary Ann,
Pray state your reason for letting this man
Wind up your clock and leave me on the shelf.
If your clock wants winding I'll wind it myself.'

Now this German grew bolder, he thought he was great,
But soon he got kicked right off the estate,
Never again in the course of his life
To wind up the clock of another man's wife.

⚜ · *IT WAS IN AN* · ⚜ AUSTRIAN LAGER

Singing was an important recreation, and hence safety valve, for prisoners-of-war. Their repertoire was similar to that of other soldiers of their time, except that it included a few songs relating to prison camp life. The Stoke prisoners sang both 'Suvla Bay' (or its Second World War update, 'Suda Bay') and a parody, perhaps of their own composition.

Tune: 'Suvla Bay'

It was in an Austrian *Lager* with a pisshole by the door;
The *Gefangener* stood waiting for the finish of the war.
With the flies all buzzing round him he gave way to horrid moans,
And cursed the bleeding Führer: 'May the devil have his bones.'
(Chorus)
Why do we work and toil all day when we could sleep so far away?
We played our part, forgot to run, and we got caught by a bleeding Hun.

Members of a working party of British prisoners-of-war at Gestuthof, Austria, during the Second World War

⤏ · BELLA CIAO · ⤎

A song from the repertoire of the paddy-field workers of Lombardy was adopted and adapted by anti-fascist partisans, and became popular with Italians resisting the German take-over of their country after the fall of Mussolini in 1943. It has been suggested that '*Bella Ciao*' was sung after the resistance struggle of 1943–5 rather than during it. However, the Stoke prisoners' experience contradicts this, for they learnt the song in 1943 while working in the fields alongside Italian peasants. Nearly thirty years later they still remembered it.

Stamattina mi son alzato,
(Chorus)
Bella ciao, bella ciao, bella ciao, ciao, ciao,
Stamattina mi son alzato
E ho trovato l'invasor.

O partigiano, portami via . . .
Che mi sento di morir.

E se murio da partigiano . . .
Tu mi devi seppelli.

E seppellire lassù in montagna . . .
Sotto l'ombra di un bel fior.

E le genti che passeranno . . .
E diranno: 'O che bel fior'.

'È questo il fiore del partigiano . . .
Morto per la libertà'.

[This morning I got up . . .
And found the invader here.

O partisan take me away . . .
Because I feel as if I am dying.

And if I die as a partisan . . .
You must bury me.

Bury me in the mountains . . .
In the shade of a fine flower.

And those who pass by . . .
Will say: 'What a fine flower.

'This is the flower of the partisan . . .
Who died for liberty.']

⋘ · *RINGERANGEROO* · ⋙

In a fifteenth-century poem François Villon caused his famous fair armouress to ask what had become of the beauties of her youth, of:

> *Ces larges rains, ce sadinet*
> *Assis sur grosses fermes cuisses,*
> *Dedens son petit jardinet.*

> These wide loins, that treasure
> Set over full, firm thighs
> In its little garden.

It is surely not fanciful to see an echo in another erotic song which, although uncommon in print, is known from Britain to North America and the West Indies under titles like 'Rackyman Doo' and 'Ringrangroo'. The version given here comes again from the Stoke-on-Trent men.

> Now as I was walking out one day
> I met a sweet girl by the way.
> I said: 'Hello. How do you do?'
> She said: 'You'd like to play with my ringerangeroo.'

> 'Your ringerangeroo,' I said, 'what's that?'
> She said: 'It's soft like a pussy cat,
> With hair all round, and cut in two;
> That's what I call my ringerangeroo.'

> She took me to her father's cellar.
> She said: 'You are a nice young feller.'
> She gave me wine and whisky too,
> And I played around with her ringerangeroo.

> Just then her dad he came and said:
> 'I'm afraid you've lost your maidenhead.
> So take a trip and your luggage too,
> And go and live on your ringerangeroo.'

> She went to town, set up as a whore.
> She hung this sign outside her door:
> 'Five dollars down, or less will do,
> When you come to play with my ringerangeroo.'

The fellers came, the fellers went.
The price dropped down to cinquante cent.
From sweet sixteen to ninety-two
They played around with her ringerangeroo.

Her ringerangeroo is sadly worn,
Her ringerangeroo is badly torn.
Let's say goodbye now, bid a fond adieu,
Let's say goodbye to her ringerangeroo.

· THEY SAY THERE'S · A BOAT ON THE RIVER

Grousing is supposed to have been a perennial safety valve for British soldiers. (During my national service in the 1950s it was known as 'ticking'.) This kind of song lent itself to various complaints: there are no doubt verses in addition to those given here. The second verse derives from the cavalry between the wars, but that did not prevent its being sung by the infantrymen of Stoke-on-Trent during their time in prisoner-of-war camps during the Second World War.

Tune: 'Follow the Band'

They say there's a boat on the river, the river,
They say that it's loaded with beer.
Oh why is that boat on the river, the river?
It fucking well ought to be here.
(*Chorus*)
Singing, aye jig a jig, fuck a little pig, follow the band,
Follow the band all the way.

I've been in the saddle for hours and hours,
I've stuck it as long as I could.
I stuck it, I stuck it, and then I said 'Fuck it.
My arsehole is not made of wood.'

ᴄᴇᴇ · THE GAY · ᴂᴅ CABALLERO

George Coppard remembered this mock-cautionary tale from the First World War, the Stoke-on-Trent prisoners-of-war from the Second. The song was also known in America.

Now there once was a gay caballero
Who strolled through the streets of Palmiro,
Flashing the whole of his wonderful, wonderful,
(*Chorus*)
Toora lye oora lye ay.

Now he met a gay señorita,
An exceedingly gay señorita,
And he showed her the whole of his wonderful, *etc.*

So she took him to her haciendo,
An exceedingly large haciendo,
And she played with the whole, *etc.*

So they lay down upon the sofito,
An exceedingly springy sofito,
And he put in the end of his wonderful, *etc.*

Now he's got a dose of clapito,
An exceedingly large dose of clapito,
Right on the end of his, *etc.*

So he went to see a surgeono,
An exceedingly great surgeono,
Who cut off the end of his, *etc.*

Now this bold and the brave caballero
Still strolls through the streets of Palmiro,
Flashing what's left of his, *etc.*

 · DOWN THE MINE ·

Among the many camps in which the Japanese held British prisoners during the Second World War was Kinkaseki, on the north-eastern coast of Taiwan (then called Formosa). The men marched to work each day in a copper mine. On the way, to overcome boredom and fatigue and to offer discreet defiance to their captors, they sang. This song, by a fellow prisoner, Arthur Smith of Leven, Fife, is remembered still by Maurice ('Mick') Rooney (now aged sixty-nine) of Norwich. As a young member of 288 Field Company, RE, Rooney was involved in the mass surrender ordered by the British commander at Singapore in 1942. He remained a prisoner at Kinkaseki until 1945. *Bunsho dono* in the song means 'camp commander', and a *chunkle* was a sort of pick or mattock.

There's a song in old Formosa that the Nips they loudly sing;
In the billets every evening you should hear the music ring.
Now they sing to British soldiers who've travelled from afar
To fight for king and country – now they're prisoners-of-war,
But they know they'll see their homeland in the future once again:
Listen while I sing to you the Nipponese refrain.
(*Chorus*)
Down the mine, bonny laddies, down the mine you'll go.
Though your feet are lacerated you did not answer, 'no';
Though the rice is insufficient and we treat you all like swine,
Down the mine, bonny laddies, down the mine.

Now the boys were fairly happy till one cold and cloudy day
When the *bunsho dono* he came out and he to them did say:
'Now I expect you all are wondering why you're out on this parade.
The reason is you must be taught the Taiwan serenade.'

You should see us work with *chunkles*, and we work with baskets too.
Though the method is old-fashioned to the boys it's something new,
And we work away with patience till the dawn of freedom's day,
But until then the Nippon men will all be heard to say.

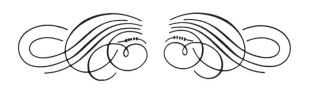

CHAPTER FOUR

SOLDIERING

About half this book is concerned with songs showing trained soldiers serving in garrisons round the world, fighting in wars, and occupying themselves in off-duty hours. Geographically, the coverage ranges from the Far East, through India and Africa to Europe. Chronologically, about a century of soldiering is covered, starting from the 1870s. Of course, some songs survived only for short periods, while others continued to be sung by generation after generation of servicemen.

When training is over, and the normal round of military life begins, soldiers' complaints at conditions continue much as before. Tickler, a manufacturer of jam during the First World War, is immortalised in several songs, and is mentioned far more often than generals or national leaders. The discomforts of the trenches at times loom larger than their horrors. Songs like 'Grousing'* are fatalistic rather than indignant, but the words 'Roll on till my time is up and I shall grouse no more' come from the heart. The phrase 'roll on' was used in exactly the same sense during my service, when every conscript had a calendar on which he crossed off the days in the countdown to his release.

Service in India inspired a body of song, including, of course, 'Bless 'em All',* with its vision of a troopship leaving Bombay. William Blackmore, a clerk in the Devonshire Regiment, produced during his time in India in the 1930s a manuscript book of songs, poems and jokes. (After his death – he did not survive the Second World War – it was passed to his sweetheart, and thus was preserved.) It contains versions of traditional songs like 'McCaffery'* and '[The Young Soldier] Cut Down',* together with poems copied from Robert Service and Rudyard Kipling, and others presumably written by Blackmore himself, such as 'Almost Time X':

> From civvies to a uniform I did exchange
> To fire a course on an open range,
> To live the life of a soldier, none better,
> Soldiering in India at a place called Quetta.
>
> From Sandeman to Wana our way we did wend,
> Eight months of our time at Razmak to spend;
> Soon on to Mari Indus our way we shall go,
> Then on to Calcutta on the plains down below.
>
> From there to Lucknow we will spend
> The last of our service abroad to defend,
> And no more stations in India I'll see,
> For it's drawing the dole in England for me.
>
> So these few lines to a close I shall draw,
> For the shores of India will see me no more.[58]

Blackmore was fascinated – and, it has to be said, repelled – by India. One poem celebrates the Taj Mahal, 'symbol sublime of an emperor's love', but most complain – at the climate, the dirt and the disease ('flies, fever and flu'). Indians are ungrateful, treacherous, dirty. Blackmore, sensitive and decent though he clearly was, was critical of the tyranny of army life while accepting the imperialist role of the army. Clive Branson, in 1942, wrote angrily of the anti-Indian sentiments of 'those bloody idiots in the regular army who want to indulge in abuse of the Indians [and who] treat the Indians in a way which not only makes one tremble for the future but which makes one ashamed of being one of them'.[59]

It is curious that the soldier accepted the outlook of his superiors towards the army's role, while rejecting it in most other respects. Healthy scepticism, not to say sardonic levelling, characterised his views of NCOs, officers and governments. His attitudes, at least as expressed in song, were at once deeply apolitical and profoundly class conscious. He longed in peace for the expiry of his time; in war, for the end of hostilities.

The rigours of war were nevertheless a favourite topic for soldier song-writers. 'D-Day Dodgers',* by Lance-Sergeant Harry Pynn, has been mentioned in the Introduction. 'The Valley of Jarama',* which expresses the weariness of the front-line soldier, was written by Alex McDade, a former regular army man fighting as a volunteer in the Spanish Civil War. The skirmish described in Hamish Henderson's 'Ballad of Wadi Maktilla'* shows the chaotic, unpleasant and inconsequential nature of much combat. Although Henderson was an officer he firmly aligned himself with the outlook of ordinary soldiers, and chose to write in traditional modes.

In many cases, authorship has not been recorded, though there is no doubt that the songs were written, either individually or collectively, by members of the rank and file. The tone varies greatly, from the triumphal to the jolly or the sorrowful. Sentimental songs have a great appeal for soldiers, even if, like 'Break the News to Mother',* they are of civilian composition. Almost universally known among soldiers were various songs of tender mothers and loving sweethearts, but these stood side by side with exaltations of the joys of sex and warnings of the dangers of venereal disease.

As one would expect from men in large numbers who were deprived for long periods of women's company, their view of women was frequently that of the sex objects of feminist demonology. The language used is often crude, as in 'Lulu',* but even here one finds a strange mixture of the coarse and the euphemistic. 'Watch and Chain Song',* like many a schoolboy chant, draws its humour from the repeated avoidance at the last moment of words transparently expected from the rhymes. On the other hand, the words avoided here are used quite deliberately elsewhere.

It is hardly surprising that homecoming is the dream and desire of most soldiers. Some men did feel a certain regret at leaving military life, as in 'Spud Spedding's Broken Boys',* though even here the title suggests a certain ambivalence. Disenchantment is squarely stated in 'The '39–'45 Star'* and 'I Don't Want My Name on a Cenotaph',* with its repetition of 'I'll be the first on the last parade'.

After 1945 soldiers continued to sing the songs of earlier times. 'Seven Nights

Drunk',* for example, dates back to the eighteenth century. They also made or adapted songs about such things as the Korean War, service in postwar Germany, and the troubles in Northern Ireland. The book concludes with the plaint in song of two army wives at the stresses which modern army life places on those married to soldiers.

A PONTOON WALLAH GOES HOME

A soldier stood at the pearly gate,
His face was scarred and old.
He stood before the man of fate
For admission to the fold.

'What have you done,' St Peter asked,
'To gain admission here?'
'I've been a soldier, sir,' he said,
'For many and many a year.'

The pearly gate swung open wide
As Peter touched the bell.
'Inside', he said, 'and choose your harp.
You've had your share of hell.'

The 2nd Battalion, Border Regiment, on manoeuvres in the Transvaal, 1906

☙ · CRE SONG · ❧

Many generations of sappers sang this marching song, which is sometimes known as 'The Royal Engineers' Whisper' because of the inclusion of a prolonged 'shhhhsh' before the final shout. The earliest versions mention Pretoria, which means that they probably date from the Boer, or even the Zulu War. Others mention Mandalay, which points to the Second World War. Still others have Laffensplain, near Aldershot, which suggests that the song was used during training.

One 'Pretoria' version was adopted by sailors as a shanty, with this chorus: 'We are marching to Pretoria, oh gloria, Victoria. We are marching to Pretoria. Victoria rules the waves.'

Oh, good morning, Mr Stevens, we've been working very hard,
Sing hurrah for the CRE;
We've been working very hard on the dingy pontoon hard,
Sing hurrah for the CRE.
Oh, you make fast, I'll make fast, make fast the dingy,
Make fast the dingy, make fast the dingy.
You make fast, I'll make fast, make fast the dingy,
Make fast the dingy tonight,
For we're marching on Pretoria, Pretoria, Pretoria,
Oh, we're marching on Pretoria,
Where they don't know sugar from
Tissue paper, tissue paper, marmalade and jam.
Oh, I saw a nigger boy sitting by a fire,
I saw a nigger boy playing with his
Hold him down while the dingy's blowing,
Hold him down till I get there.
(*Shout*) Oh, oh, oh, oh, oh, oh, oh.

· THE SOLDIER'S · RETURN – I

The emphasis on a soldier's love for his mother is typical of a number of late Victorian and Edwardian songs (and this one may date from the Egyptian War of 1882). So, too, the phraseology, with expressions like 'sunburnt face', 'silent grave' and 'like a child he cried'.

A soldier just returned again, back from a foreign shore,
Along the plains of Egypt, in a land so far away.
Upon the field of battle he'd seen his comrades fall;
There were none to welcome him, they were all dead and gone.
(*Chorus*)
Just as the bells were ringing upon that sabbath morn,
He knocked at the door of the cot where he was born.
His heart was nearly broken when a neighbour to him said:
'She's sleeping over yonder, there; my lad, your mother's dead.'

His sunburnt face grew pale as upward he bent his way,
Up to the village churchyard there, where his dear mother lay;
And kneeling down by her silent grave and like a child he cried,
And whispered: 'Soon I shall be sleeping by your side.'

· A BRITISH SOLDIER'S · GRAVE

The central emotion here is that of affection for a comrade, though love for a mother and a sweetheart also figure. The language and sentiments belong to an age altogether more innocent than our own. The song, which comes from the repertoire of the Copper family, was sung until 1896 at the annual performances of the mummers' play at Rottingdean, Sussex.

The battle it was over and the stars did brightly shine.
The moon shone o'er the dying and the dead,
And not a sound was heard save the screams of some wild bird
As it fluttered round the dying soldier's head;
And on that spot there lay one who'd nobly fought that day.
His comrade true to him was standing near,
And with an anguished sigh to his comrade gently cried,
And with his hand he wiped away a tear.
(*Chorus*)
Then he whispered goodbye to his comrade so dear,
His head upon his knapsack gently laid:
'If you live to get home you can tell them I am gone.
I'm lying in a British soldier's grave.'

'Oh don't you remember that dear old oak tree?
With my knife I cut my name out in the bark,
And early in the morn I have reaped the golden corn,
And listened to the warbling of the lark.
That dear old shady spot it shall never be forgot,
For 'twas there I used to meet the girl I love.
Tell her not to cry for I'll meet her by and by
In a brighter and better land above.

'Tell my aged mother that she's not to weep for me,
For in the battle I took a noble part.
Break it gently to her all the news, my comrade dear;
I fear that it will almost break her heart.
Tell my sister, too, I have kept the gift so dear
In parting which she fondly gave to me;
Although I still possess it I have stained with my life's blood
This dear locket was a parting gift to me.

'I feel that I am dying and my breath is going fast.
Just raise me up once more that I might see
The moon that gives us light and the watch-fires burning bright,
And my comrades as happy as can be.
There now, goodbye,' he cried. He then fell back and died,
Beloved by all, so noble and so brave;
And early the next day he beneath the turf did lay
In a rude but a British soldier's grave.

· BREAK THE NEWS TO · MOTHER

This tear-jerker of 1897, by Charles Russell Harris, was a favourite with British soldiers during the Boer War of 1899–1902, and remained in the repertoire of some singers until at least the 1970s. The Victorian emphasis on love for one's mother had an enduring appeal, especially for working-class people whose families often owed their survival to the central figure of the mother. Soldiers in any case have a predilection for sentimental songs.

While shot and shell were gleaming upon the battlefield
Our boys in blue were fighting their noble flag to shield,
When a cry from our brave captain: 'Look, boys, our flag is down.
Who'll volunteer to save it from disgrace?'
'I will,' a young boy shouted, 'I'll bring it back or die.'
He sprang into the thickest of the fray;
He saved the flag but gave his young life all for his country's sake.
They brought him back and softly heard him say:
(*Chorus*)
'Break the news to mother, she knows how dear I love her.
Tell her not to wait for me for I'm not coming home.
They say there is no other can take the place of mother;
Kiss her dear sweet lips for me, and break the news to her.'

From afar a noted general who had witnessed this brave deed:
'Who saved the flag? Speak up, my lad. It was noble, brave indeed.'
'There he lies, sir,' said our captain, 'he is sinking very fast';
He slowly turned away to hide a tear.
The general in a moment knelt down beside the boy,
He gave a cry which touched all hearts that day:
'It is my son, my brave young hero. I thought you were safe at home.'
'Forgive me, father, for I ran away.'

A picquet of the Gloucestershire Regiment at Waggon Hill, Ladysmith,
during the Boer War

· DOIN' MY DUTY ·

The irreverent attitudes which find expression in this vernacular piece contrast markedly with the patriotic pieties of 'Break the News to Mother' and 'A British Soldier's Grave', even though it is of the same vintage. The singer, Ted Cobbin of Great Glemham in Norfolk, had it from his cousin, Ross Eagle, who in turn learnt it from a Boer War veteran while serving in the RAMC.

How can England be in danger? Is there any chance of war?
You talk about your fighting men and you quite forget our corps.
You talk about your Wellingtons that fought at Waterloo,
But how about your humble on the field of Pinkypoo?
Yes, I was doin' my duty, a-doin' my duty,
Where the bullets were flying as thick as the mud
I was shedding my drops of blood,
Fighting with the corporal in the ammunition van,
Yes, I was doin' my duty like a soldier and a man.

Now you think we're under canvas, what a pleasant time was spent,
Especially when there's fifty of you bunged into a tent.
There's a dozen pairs of bluchers a-layin' all around,
But what a rush for trousers when the enemy he is found.
Yes, I'll be doin' my duty, a-doin' my duty,
Soon as ever a flea pops out his head
I give 'im a bash with a loaf of bread,
And then the bloomin' tent was like the Battle of Sedan,
For I was doin' my duty like a soldier and a man.

Now every Sunday night when I go out with my best tunic dress,
A twopenny cigar is in my mouth and a loaf stuck up my chest.
I'm chasin' bits o' calico as soon as it gets dark,
But I've always got my eye upon the benches in the park.
Yes, I'll be doin' my duty, a-doin' my duty,
A-swinging my regimental stick,
Making myself look a bit thick,
And when the moon it goes out of sight, with Flo and Mary Ann
Oh I'll be doin' my duty like a soldier and a man.

(b) The First World War

I LEARNED TO WASH IN SHELL-HOLES

I learned to wash in shell-holes and to shave myself in tea,
While the fragments of a mirror did a balance on my knee;
I learned to dodge the whizzbangs and the flying lumps of lead,
And to keep a foot of earth between the snipers and my head.

I learned to keep my haversack well filled with buckshee food,
To take my army issue and to pinch what else I could;
I learned to cook Maconochie with candle ends and string,
With four-by-two and sardine oil and any old darn thing.

I learned to use my bayonet according, as you please,
For a bread-knife or a chopper or a prong for toasting cheese;
I learned to gather souvenirs that home I hoped to send,
And hump them round for months and months and dump them in the end.

I never used to grumble after breakfast in the line
That the eggs were cooked too lightly or the bacon cut too fine;
I never told the sergeant just exactly what I thought;
I never did a pack-drill for I never quite got caught.
I never stopped a whizzbang though I've stopped a lot of mud,
But the one that Fritz sent over with my name on was a dud.

George Coppard (seated) and his uncle. Coppard (see Introduction) added three to his sixteen years of age to join the Royal West Kent Regiment in 1914

ᐸᑕ · GROUSING · ᑌᐳ

A somewhat lugubrious hymn was parodied in this marching song. 'Lousing' or 'boozing' was sometimes substituted for 'grousing' in verse one. Both 'grousing' and 'grooming' have been reported from versions sung by horsemen during the Boer War. The war-weary message of the song was recognised in some cases during the First World War by its 'being sternly suppressed by company commanders, where men have spent long hours on the march, as being detrimental to good discipline'.

Tune: 'Holy, holy, holy'

Grousing, grousing, grousing, always blooming well grousing. } *bis*
Roll on till my time is up and I shall grouse no more.

Raining, raining, raining, always bally well raining, } *bis*
Raining all the morning and raining all the night.

Marching, marching, marching, always ruddy well marching. } *bis*
Roll on till my time is up and I shall march no more.

ᐸᑕ · WE ARE BUT LITTLE · ᑌᐳ SEAFORTHS WEAK

In this case the tune of a Methodist children's hymn is chosen as a vehicle for complaints about low pay, overwork and lack of leave. A version of the first verse at least was sung during the Boer War, and others ('We are the little ASC' and 'We are but little soldiers weak') during the First World War. The text given here was noted by Ewart MacIntosh, himself a skilful writer of parodies, with these comments: 'I am indebted for this lyric to the privates of No. 16 Platoon of my Battalion. I don't know how many survive of the composers, but I record my thanks to them.' MacIntosh was killed himself, at Cambrai, in 1917.

Tune: 'We are but little children weak'

We are but little Seaforths weak,
Our pay is seven bob a week.
Whate'er we do by night or day,
It makes no difference to our pay.

Our hours a day are twenty-four.
We thank the lord there are no more,
For if there were we know that we
Would work another two or three.

There is one thing we do believe,
That we're entitled to some leave.
We know not why we are so cursed,
We'll get our old-age pensions first.

ⅭⒼ · *WE BEAT 'EM ON THE* · ⅭⒼ MARNE

Battles took place on the Marne in 1914, on the Aisne in 1914, 1917 and 1918 (though the first is probably intended here), and at Neuve Chapelle in 1915. This marching song is less an expression of combativeness than of the ability to endure.

Tune: 'Coming Through the Rye'

We beat 'em on the Marne,
We beat 'em on the Aisne;
They gave us hell at Neuve Chapelle,
But here we are again.

ᴄ⳨ꙅ · *NEUVE CHAPELLE* · ꙅ⳨ᴏ

Neuve Chapelle is a French village to the west of Lille. A British offensive there in March 1915 took the village from the Germans but failed to capture the ridge. In three days there were 12,000 casualties. The song is therefore perhaps unduly cheerful. It was composed by a sergeant of the 27th Division, and became a favourite of the Inniskillings or Irish Rifles, who sang it when leaving the trenches or in *estaminets*.

General von Kluck, who is mentioned, commanded the German 1st Army in the early stages of the war. He was defeated at the Marne in September 1914, and retired the following year. His name readily lent itself to disrespectful rhymes, as in this, to the tune of 'Brighton Camp':

> Now a soldier's life is a merry life, it is when he's not tramping.
> We'll take a trip to Aldershot and watch the boys a-camping.
> Now Brighton Camp has just broke up, it was so wet and slimy,
> I stuck my head up a nanny goat's arse and the stink was enough to blind me.
> Oh Kaiser Bill is feeling ill, the Crown Prince he's gone barmy,
> And we don't give a fuck for old von Kluck and all his fucking army.

Rather more affectionate was an item Robert Graves heard, to the tune of 'Old Macdonald had a farm':

> Now old von Kluck he had a lot of men, ee-aye-ee-aye-oh!
> And every man he had a little gun, eee-aye-ee-aye-oh!
> With a ping-ping here and a ping-ping there,
> And here a ping, there a ping, ping-pinging everywhere,
> It's old von Kluck he had a lot of men, ee-aye-ee-aye-oh!

Tune: 'The Rambling Irishman'

> For when we landed in Belgium the girls all danced with joy;
> Says one unto the other, 'Here comes an Irish boy.'
> Then it's fare thee well, dear mother, we'll do the best we can,
> For you all know that Neuve Chapelle was won by an Irishman.

(*Chorus*)
Then here's good luck to the Rifles, the Inniskillings, too;
The Royal Irish Fusiliers and the Royal Artillery, too;
For side by side they fought and died as noble heroes can,
And you all know well that Neuve Chapelle was won by an Irishman.

Said von Kluck unto the Kaiser, 'What are we going to do?
We're going to meet those Irishmen, the men we never knew.'
Says the Kaiser unto old von Kluck, 'We'll do the best we can,
But I'm telling you true that Waterloo was won by an Irishman.'

⳾ · *SUVLA BAY* · ⳾

The song takes its title from a place on the western side of the Dardanelles Peninsula where an ANZAC force landed in August 1915. By coincidence an action took place at Suda Bay in Crete in May 1941, after which a defeated Allied force surrendered to the Germans. The earlier song was quickly adapted as 'Suda Bay', and both British and Australians sang it. It acquired the reputation of being forbidden: one Australian stated that 'you can get arrested for singing that song'. Reg Baker of Stoke-on-Trent, who surrendered at Suda Bay, sang the song in German prison camps, but Gordon Hall's version of the original words is given here.

In an old Australian homestead with the roses round the door
A girl received a letter sent to her from the war.
With her mother's arms around her she began to sob and sigh;
As she read that sad, sad letter the tears bedimmed her eye.
(*Chorus*)
Why do I weep, who do I pray? My love's asleep so far away.
He played his part that August day, and left my heart at Suvla Bay.

Then she joined a band of sisters beneath a cross of red,
Just to try to do her duty to her sweetheart who lay dead.
Many fellows came to woo her but were sadly turned away
When she told them the sad, sad story of her love on Suvla Bay.

ᘓ · *SALONIKA* · ᘔ

The Greek port of Salonika came to prominence in 1915 when it was used to mount and supply the Gallipoli expeditionary force. The song, though, is concerned with what the soldiers will find when they return home. It probably originated in Cork, but became known in the British Army (many of whose members were in any case Irish, especially during the First World War). The verse mentioning Sinn Fein was no doubt a later addition.

Oh me husband's in Salonika, I wonder if he's dead.
I wonder if he knows he's got a kid with a poxy head.
(*Chorus*)
So right away, right away,
Right away, Salonika, right away,
My soldier boy.

Well, when the war is over,
What will the soldiers do?
They'll be walking around with a leg in their hand;
The slackers they'll have two.

Well, when the war is over
What will the slackers do?
They'll be hanging around the soldier boys
For the loan of a bob or two.

Well, they've taxed the pound of butter,
They've taxed the penny bun,
But still with all their taxes
They can't beat the bloody Hun.

Now when the war is over
What will the slackers do?
For every kid in America
In Cork there will be two.

Well, they've taxed the Coliseum,
They've taxed St Mary's Hall.
Why don't they tax the gombeens
With their backs against the wall?

Well, they take us out to Blarney
And they lay us on the grass.
They put us in the family way
And they leave us on our arse.

Well, never trust a soldier,
A sailor or a marine,
And keep your eye on the Sinn Fein boy
With his orange, white and green.

ℰ · *NEVER MIND* · ℰ

Here, soldiers appropriated the chorus of a sentimental song of 1913 by Harry Dent
and Tom Goldburn, which ran:

Though your heart may ache awhile, never mind!
Though your face may lose its smile, never mind!
For there's sunshine after rain, and then gladness follows pain.
You'll be happy once again, never mind.

Not surprisingly, the parody was rather more cynical.

Tune: 'Never Mind'

If the sergeant drinks your rum, *never mind*;
And your face may lose its smile, *never mind*.
He's entitled to a tot but not the bleeding lot,
If the sergeant drinks your rum, *never mind*.

When old Jerry shells your trench, *never mind* (*bis*).
Though the sandbags bust and fly you have only once to die,
If old Jerry shells the trench, *never mind*.

If you get stuck on the wire . . .
Though you're stuck there all the day, they count you dead and stop your pay.

If the sergeant says you're mad . . .
P'raps you are a little bit . . .
Just be calm, don't answer back, 'cause the sergeant stands no 'slack',
So if he says you're mad, well – you are.

ᴄᴇ · *TICKLER'S JAM* · ᴇᴏ

Tickler's jam was widely used by the army, especially during the early years of the First World War. According to popular belief it was made, as Walter Bunn of Birmingham put it, 'of mangel wurzels and swedes, flavoured with plum juice, and sweetened'. He added: 'You didn't need a knife and fork to get it out of the tins: you simply poured it out.' (Bunn was in the army from 1904 until 1918, and died in 1989, just after his 103rd birthday.) The singer here was George Coppard, author of *With a Machine Gun to Cambrai* (1969).

Tickler's jam, Tickler's jam, how I love old Tickler's jam.
Plum and apple in a one-pound pot, sent from Blighty in a ten-ton lot.
Every night when I'm asleep I'm dreaming that I am
Forcing my way through the Dardanelles with a ton of Tickler's jam.

ᴄᴇ · *ODE TO TICKLER* · ᴇᴏ

A further ironic tribute to Tickler's jam also brings in 'bully' (corned beef, from '*boeuf bouilli*') and 'Maconochie' (tinned vegetable stew, from the name of its inventor).

Tune: 'Sweet Genevieve'

Oh jam for tea, oh jam for tea,
I'm jolly sure it don't suit me;
I've tried for years and now in tears
I'll sing it to you mournfully.

Oh jam for tea, oh jam for tea,
The world knows how you've tortured me;
I've frills and squills, you've made me bills,
And filled the dentists' empty tills.

Oh jam for tea, oh jam for tea,
Fried bully and Maconochie;
But when we get back to Blighty-y-y-y
We will have ham and lamb for tea.

Arthur Wilding of Felsham, Suffolk, c. 1916

ᘓᕉ · PLUM AND APPLE · ᖇᕩ

'Is it plum and apple?' 'No, it's apple and plum.' The weary joke reflected the ubiquity of plum and apple jam during the First World War. So did the Bairnsfather cartoon. So did the songs both of the trenches (A) and the music hall (B).

A. Tune: 'A Wee Deoch and Doris'
Plum and apple, apple and plum,
Plum and apple, there is always some.
The ASC get strawberry jam and lashings of rum,
But we poor blokes we only get apple and plum.

B.
When first the boys in khaki went away to win the war,
The food out there was great, I'm very glad to state,
They'd ev'ry kind of luxury, they'd mutton, beef and lamb,
They'd also twenty million tins of plum and apple jam.
They all ate plum and apple till they'd got it on the brain,
And ev'ry Tommy in the trenches now sings this refrain
Each evening:
(*Chorus*)
Plum and apple, apple and plum!
Jam for breakfast, jam for tea;
But we never get a bit of strawberry.
Plum and apple, till the boys begin to say,
If we'd used those tins of jam, you see,
As shells for our artillery,
We'd have won this war quite easily,
And been in Berlin today.

When Sergeant Binns came home on leave he found to his surprise
His wife, Matilda Binns, had presented him with twins.
He gazed on the youngsters and his heart was filled with joy,
A darling little girl and such a bonny little boy.
'What shall we call them?' said his wife. 'I'll leave the names to you.'
'I don't like fancy names,' said Binns. 'I'll tell you what we'll do.
We'll call them . . .

Now Private Mick Maloney of the Dublin Fusiliers
Got wounded out in France in the British big advance;
They brought him home to hospital, and whilst in bed he lay,
A lady who liked asking silly questions called one day.
'What brought you here, Maloney? Was it poison gas?' she cried.
'Or was it shells?' But with a wink Maloney then replied:
'No, it was . . .'

Byatander copyright.

THE ETERNAL QUESTION
"When the 'ell is it goin' to be strawberry?"

Cartoon by Bruce Bairnsfather

· BULLY AND JAM ·

In France during the First World War the inevitability of corned beef and jam in the soldiers' diet provided ample opportunities for humorous comment. The song was written in 1918 by F. A. Todd, a soldier in the Australian Army who returned safely and became Professor of English at Sydney University.

Tune: 'Chantons l'Artillerie'

We chorus as we're marching along
In warm or wintry weather
A rousing, roaring company song,
And beef it out together.
Bully and jam for dinner,
Come rain or sun or snow.
Bully and jam for tea,
Jam, jam, bully and jam for tea.
Bully and jam for dinner,
Come rain or sun or snow,
Bully and jam for tea.

We battened once on turkey and ham
In days we've nigh forgotten,
But now we live on bully and jam,
And find 'em none so rotten.
Tramp, tramping day and night,
Bully and jam for dinner,
Lord, we've an appetite,
Bully and jam for tea,
Jam, jam, bully and jam for tea.
Bully and jam for dinner,
Lord, we've an appetite,
Bully and jam for tea.

The sergeant and the C in C,
The colonel and the digger
Find army grub for dinner and tea
Improving to the figure,
So as we tramp along,
Bully and jam for dinner,
We sing a cheery song, *etc.*

And wheresoe'er the company come,
To camp or trench or billet,
We sing a song of the company tum
And the bully and jam that fill it.
Boys, as we tramp along,
Bully and jam for dinner,
This be our marching song, *etc.*

Ꮼ · *FRAY MARIE* · Ꮼ

A Belgian brothel – should it be 'Chez Marie'? – or rather one of its ladies is celebrated in a song sung during both World Wars by British and Australian soldiers and sailors.

Tune: 'Down Home in Tennessee'

Way down in Fray Marie
Ten francs I paid to see
A French tattooed lady,
Tattooed from head to knee.
On her left jaw
Was the Royal Flying Corps,
And on her back
Was the Union Jack.
Could anyone ask for more?

And up and down her spine
Are the Coldstream Guards in line,
And on her shapely hips
Is a fleet of battleships.
Tattooed on each kidney
Is a bird's-eye view of Sydney.
Around the corner,
The Johnny Horner,
My girl from Battersea.

☙ · THREE GERMAN · ❧ OFFICERS CROSSED THE RHINE

Johann Ludwig Uhland (1787–1862) wrote a series of ballads which enjoyed great success; a collection of them published under the title of *Vaterländische Gedichte* went into over fifty editions in his lifetime alone. One of the pieces, '*Der Wirtin Töchterlein*' ('The Landlady's Little Daughter'), tells how three German soldiers crossed the Rhine to visit an inn. They ask the landlady about her beer and wine, and then enquire after her daughter. In response, she takes them to a bedroom and shows them the girl's dead body. Each then declares that he was in love with her daughter.

Parodists soon gratefully appropriated the sentimental text, and replaced the eighteenth-century tune by others. It is not clear when the English words first appeared, but the parody was popular with American soldiers who learnt it from the British during the First World War. Canadians took it up, too. There are many versions, but these seldom appear in print, other than in bowdlerised form. The text given here was learnt by Gordon Hall from two men with a great fund of First World War songs, who were his workmates in the 1940s at a Sussex chemical factory.

The song's popularity with the troops no doubt lies in the avid sexuality displayed by most of the protagonists.

Tune: 'Mademoiselle from Armentières'

> Three German officers crossed the Rhine, *taboo, taboo,*
> Three German officers crossed the Rhine, *taboo.*
> Three German officers crossed the Rhine
> To fuck the women and drink the wine.
> (*Chorus*)
> *Taboo, tabye, tabollocky eye, taboo.*
>
> They came to the door of a wayside inn,
> Pissed on the mat and walked right in.
>
> 'Oh landlord, have you a daughter fair
> With lily-white tits and golden hair?'
>
> 'My only daughter's far too young
> To be fucked by you, you bastard Hun.'
>
> 'Oh father, dear, I'm not too young,
> I've just been fucked by the blacksmith's son.'

At last they got her on the bed,
And shagged her till her cheeks were red.

And then they took her to a bed,
And shagged her till she was nearly dead.

They took her down a shady lane,
Shagged her back to life again.

They shagged her up, they shagged her down,
They shagged her all around the town.

They shagged her in, they shagged her out,
They shagged her up a water spout.

Now seven months later and all was well;
Eight months later she started to swell.

Nine months later she gave a grunt,
And a little fat Prussian popped out of her cunt.

This fat little Prussian he grew and grew;
He fucked the cat and the donkey, too.

The fat little Prussian he went to hell;
He shagged the devil and his wife as well.

· I'LL BE THERE ·

A number of writers who served in the First World War, including Edmund Blunden, mention this song, which was sung both on the march and when soldiers were off duty.

Tune: 'When the Roll is Called up Yonder'

> When the stew is on the table, (*ter*)
> (*Chorus*)
> *I'll be there, I'll be there, I'll be there.*
>
> When the beer is in the tankard, *etc.*
>
> When there's pay parade on Friday, *etc.*

· *I WANT TO GO HOME* ·

From winter 1915 until summer 1916 W. Cushing, then in his twenties, was in the trenches of the Ypres Salient with the 9th Norfolk Regiment. He recalled:

> We sometimes went up to Ypres by train . . . yes, by train. The engine would glide silently along the single track; and provided the rails had not been smashed by shell fire, we arrived just outside Ypres, where we detrained in silence. How a steam engine could glide so noiselessly I never understood. The men also were silent, for the same reason that the engine was; not to attract unwanted attention from the enemy's batteries, but also from a sad and mournful apprehension. Nevertheless, I remember one night, a night as still and silent as the engine and the men, when someone started to sing *sotto voce* that haunting, nostalgic cry, taken up by all: 'Oh my, I don't want to die, I want to go home.' I can still hear that murmured wish and longing. These men were not the heroes for whom homes were to be provided after the war that was to end wars: they were boys who wanted to go home. I wonder how many had their wish.

Literary combatants in the First World War frequently remark on the song, one of the most famous of the time. Robert Graves oddly calls it 'defeatist', while C. E. Montague describes it as 'one of the soldiers' contumacious songs of mock-funk'. Henry Williamson says that men cheerily sang it while walking out of camp. Ivor Gurney reports it from the trenches:

> Here is a song our men sang when the last strafe was at its hottest – a very popular song about here; but not military . . . Nor a brave song, but brave men sing it.

According to E. A. Dolph the author of the words of the song was a Canadian, Lieutenant Gitz Rice. Part of the tune is reminiscent of 'Bless 'em All'.
A Second World War version comes from 43 Squadron of the RAF:

> I want to go home, I want to go home.
> I don't want to go up the beaches no more
> Where Focke-Wolf and Eighty-eights whistle and roar.
> Take me over the sea where the Messerschmitts can't get me.
> Oh my, I'm too young to die, I want to go home.

I want to go home, I want to go home.
I don't want to go to the trenches no more,
Where whizzbangs and shrapnel they whistle and roar.
Take me over the sea where the Alleyman can't get at me.
Oh my, I don't want to die, I want to go home.

I want to go home, I want to go home,
I don't want to visit *la Belle France* no more,
For oh the Jack Johnsons they make such a roar.
Take me over the sea where the snipers they can't snipe at me.
Oh my, I don't want to die, I want to go home.

· RAGTIME SOLDIER ·

John Pearce of Birmingham was conscripted into the 2/9 Royal Warwickshire Regiment in 1916. He learned the song on the march, but was inclined to sing 'All for a tanner a day', since out of his pay of a shilling a day he allotted sixpence to his mother. The tune was adopted from a popular song of the day, 'Ragtime Lover'. Soldiers applied the adjective to 'any manifestation of insufficiency or absurdity'. Pearce was invalided out of the army in 1917 after being gassed in France, but was still alive seventy years later.

Tune: 'Ragtime Lover'

> For he's a ragtime soldier, a ragtime soldier,
> Early in the morning when he's out on parade,
> Early in the dawning with his rifle and his spade;
> For he's a ragtime soldier as happy as the flowers in May,
> He's a-fighting for his king and his country,
> All for a shilling a day.

·THERE'S A BATTALION· OUT IN FRANCE

During the Battle of the Somme in 1916, High Wood was the scene of exceptionally fierce fighting. The 16th Battalion of the King's Royal Rifle Corps, mainly made up of former members of the Church Lads' Brigade, sustained particularly severe losses. One of its soldiers, whose name has not been recorded, wrote these verses, of which 'almost every man had scribbled out a copy in his own handwriting'. Denham in Buckinghamshire is where the battalion had trained.

There's a battalion out in France, its name was spread afar,
And if you want to know its name, it's the 16th KRR.
They trained for months at Denham, which made every man quite fit,
Then on 16th November they embarked to do their bit.
The ride it was fairly long and I'm sure it was no treat,
For the only food that we could get was biscuits and bully beef.

Now the first time in the trenches it was not so very bad,
But on the second of January a lively time we had.
The shells flew all around us, yes, there were many a score,
And the only shelter we could find was to lay flat on the floor.

Of course, you know, we lost a few, which I am sorry to say,
But we will have our own back on the Allemands one day;
But still we have to carry on, of work we do our share,
And unless we have an RE fatigue you seldom hear us swear.

Now when the war is finished and we return once more,
If they take us back to Denham there will be a treat in store,
But we shall not forget the lads that we have left behind,
And we all hope they will rest in peace where the sun will always shine.

Now here's good luck to all of us no matter where we are,
For we know the name will never fade of the 16th KRR.

George Hewins of Stratford-upon-Avon and his family. Hewins (here shown on leave in 1915) served in the Warwickshire Regiment. His life story, edited by his granddaughter-in-law, Angela Hewins, was published in 1981 under the title of The Dillen

Two First World War soldiers, G. Nash and Corporal K. Thurland, pose for a photograph destined to be sent home

· THE SOLDIER'S · RETURN – II

This was written in the trenches of the First World War by a soldier whose name has not been recorded. The 'Swiss trench' (verse one) may mean 'Switch Line', one of the German positions during the Battle of the Somme in 1916.

Tune: 'The Learig'

When ower yon hills the bullets flew,
The shells they burst like fury O,
When doon yon trench in single file
We ran like hell, my dearie O.
Doon by the burn where Swiss trench lies
The nicht was dark and dreary O,
And mony's the lad nae rise again,
Nae more he'll see his dearie O.

But when the word 'Advance' was passed,
Our eyes wi sleep were bleary O.
We sang the marshallease o' France,
But Scotland yet, my dearie O.
Nae doubt the folk at hame wud muse
For gallant lads sae cheery O,
But when Germans fell like sheaves o' corn
We thocht of you, my dearie O.

When ower yon seas we'll come again,
And war nae mair, my dearie O,
And you an' I are aa oor ain,
We'll drink a cup sae cheery O;
And in auld Edinburgh toon
We'll name the day, my dearie O,
An' we like bairnies cuddle doon,
Ne hae nae cause to weary O.

ᑢᕾᕼᕽ · *HANGING ON THE* · ᕽᕼᕾᑢ
OLD BARBED WIRE

Lyn Macdonald suggests that this song, originally critical of officers and NCOs, had the bitter final verse added after the Battle of the Somme. Officers discouraged the men from singing it on the march, but it nevertheless became widely known to British and (later) American troops. It stuck in the minds of such soldier-writers as David Jones, who quoted it in his long poem, *In Parenthesis*, and J. B. Priestley, who considered it 'the best' of the songs 'sharply concerned with military life from the view-point of the disillusioned private'. Of the title phrase, Priestley added: 'To this day I cannot listen to it unmoved. There is a flash of pure genius, entirely English, in that "old", for it means that even the devilish enemy, that death-trap, the wire, has somehow been accepted, recognised and acknowledged almost with affection, by the deep rueful charity of this verse. I have looked through whole anthologies that said less to me.'

Some continued to sing the song even during the Second World War. Certainly, it was known to the Canadians, one of whose regiments, the Princess Patricia's Light Infantry – in a curious reversal of the usual flow from official to unofficial – adopted the tune as a march past.

The singer here, Gordon Hall, has several variations on the words, which are shown in brackets. Joe Driscoll (verse five) was a friend of his mother's who died in the trenches during the First World War. Another First World War soldier suggests that 'canteen' in verse two should be 'latrine', thus underlining the sergeant's alleged state of funk.

If you want to find the lance-jack, *I know where he is,*
I know where he is, I know where he is.
If you want to find the lance-jack, *I know where he is,*
He's scrounging round the cookhouse door.
I've seen him, I've seen him,
Scrounging round the cookhouse door, *I've seen him,*
Scrounging round the cookhouse door.

The company sergeant . . . He's laying on the canteen floor.
(Blind drunk on the canteen floor.)

The quarter bloke . . . Miles and miles behind the lines.

The sergeant-major . . . Thieving the squaddies' rum.
(Guzzling the squaddies' rum.)

Joe Driscoll . . . Laying on the firing step.
(With half his head blown away.)

The buckshee private . . . Buried in a deep shell hole.
(Cut to pieces by a shrapnel shell.)

The CO . . . Down in a deep dugout.

The brasshats . . . Drinking claret at brigade HQ.
(Pinning up another rooti-gong.)

The politicians . . . They're feathering their nests back home.
(Drinking brandy at the House of Commons bar.)

The whole battalion (the second battalion) . . . Hanging on the old barbed wire.
(Hanging up like washing on the line.)

*A Canadian corporal is decorated with the DCM in the field during the
First World War*

⟨⟩ · THE BOYS IN · ⟨⟩ PALESTINE

In 1916 a British force under the command of General (later Field-Marshal) Allenby set out from Egypt to invade Palestine, which had been under Turkish rule for some four hundred years. By the end of 1917 Jerusalem had been captured, and at the end of the war Palestine was placed under British control as a protectorate. Some soldiers 'from Richmond and district' expressed their revulsion to Middle Eastern campaigning in the form of a song.

Tune: 'From Greenland's Icy Mountains' (otherwise known as 'The Church's One Foundation')

> We came from Turkey's mountains to Egypt's blazing strand,
> Where Afric's sunny fountains are mostly choked with sand.
> We've seen its ancient river, we've seen its palmy plain;
> Our greatest hope is never to see the place again.
>
> We've climbed up both the pyramids, we've fished in the canal;
> If we haven't got the sunstroke no doubt in time we shall.
> They've placed us near to Suez, our heads are fit to burst,
> And we quite agree with Kipling that a man can raise a thirst.
>
> We've felt those gentle showers whose very rain is sand;
> We've seen, like Joseph's brethren, the bareness of the land.
> We've tried the plagues of Egypt, we've known the flies and lice,
> And we sympathise with Pharoah who hadn't any ice.
>
> What though the spicy breezes blow soft o'er Ceylon's isle,
> They ain't much good to us blokes who sweat beside the Nile.
> In vain with lavish kindness they issue Tickler's jam;
> We're blinking with sun-blindness and no one cares a damn.
>
> From Sidi Bishr to Kubri, from Suez to El Shatt,
> There's nothing here but niggers, each blacker than your hat.
> The sun has scorched our noses and our idea of bliss
> Is for another Moses to take us out of this.

· OH! IT'S A LOVELY · WAR

The song written in 1917 by J. P. Long and Maurice Scott was quickly taken up by the troops, the last four lines of the chorus being most likely to stick in their memories. The stage production (and later film) which took its title in the 1960s made the song widely known once more.

Up to your waist in water, up to your eyes in slush,
Using the kind of language that makes the sergeant blush,
Who wouldn't join the army? That's what we all enquire.
Don't we pity the poor civilians sitting beside the fire.
(*Chorus*)
Oh, oh, oh it's a lovely war.
Who wouldn't be a soldier, eh? Oh it's a shame to take the pay.
As soon as reveille has gone we feel just as heavy as lead,
But we never get up till the sergeant brings our breakfast up to bed.
Oh, oh, oh it's a lovely war.
What do we want with eggs and ham when we've got plum and apple jam?
Form fours. Right turn. How shall we spend the money we earn?
Oh, oh, oh it's a lovely war.

When does a soldier grumble? When does he make a fuss?
No one is more contented in all the world than us.
Oh it's a cushy life, boys, really we love it so:
Once a fellow was sent on leave and simply refused to go.

Come to the cookhouse door, boys, sniff at the lovely stew.
Who is it says the colonel gets better grub than you?
Any complaints this morning? Do we complain? Not we.
What's the matter with lumps of onion floating around the tea?

◠ · *THE LAST LONG* · ◠
MILE

Like 'Oh! It's a Lovely War', this may well be a song of civilian composition, though I have not traced its author. It was certainly taken up by the troops. The opening words seem to refer to conscription, which was introduced in the case of the First World War in 1916. The word 'Napootaloo' comes from 'napoo', a soldier's corruption of '*il n'y en a plus*', meaning, in this case, 'gone'.

They put us in the army and they handed us a pack,
They took away our nice new clothes and dressed us up in khak';
They marched us twenty miles and more to fit us for the war:
We didn't mind the nineteen but the last one made us sore.
(*First chorus*)
Oh it's not the pack that you carry on your back
Nor the gun upon your shoulder,
Nor the five-inch crust of France's dirty dust
That makes you feel your limbs are growing older.
It's not the load on the hard straight road
That drives away your smile;
If the socks of sister raise a blister
Blame it on the last long mile.

One day we had manoeuvres on dear old Salisbury Plain.
We marched and marched and marched and marched and marched and
    marched again.
I thought the Duke of York a fool but he wasn't in the van
With us who marched and marched and marched and marched back home
    again.
(*Second chorus*)
Oh it's not the pack that you carry on your back
Nor the gun upon your shoulder;
If there's never any ham there's plum and apple jam
To make you feel your limbs are growing older.
Oh it's not the camp nor the echoes of the tramp
That drives away your smile,
It's the sergeant-major's little wager
To beat you on the last long mile.

Now we've been out in Flanders for many a weary day,
A-marching and a-fighting in the good old British way.
We don't complain of nothing but we'd dearly like to know
Before we are Napootaloo what for, where to we go.
(*Third chorus*)
Oh it's not the packs that we carry on our backs
Nor the guns upon our shoulders,
And we're glad we're o'er the foam from the stay-at-homes who roam,
Although we feel our limbs are growing older.
Oh it's not the fear of France's rotten beer
That drives away our smile,
But if the British workman beats the German
We'll stick it to the last long mile.

The Worcesters going into action,
as shown in a carefully organised photograph of the First World War

∽ · *SOLDIER'S LULLABY* · ∾

The curious compound of resignation and longing, indignation and despair, make this a memorable piece. As early as 1917 Patrick MacGill quoted a short version in a collection of his own poems published under the title of *Soldier Songs*. The full text given here comes from a lady whose brothers served in the First World War. She might have learnt it from them, or alternatively from the seamstresses with whom she worked during the war in a tailoring sweatshop in the East End of London. The workers lightened their labour not only by joking and singing but by writing letters and verses to those who would be wearing the uniforms which they were making, and putting them in the pockets. The tune was taken from a sentimental ballad dating from before 1914.

Tune: 'Sing me to Sleep'

Sing me to sleep where bullets fall,
Let me forget this war and all.
Cold is my dug-out, damp my feet;
Nothing but biscuits and bully to eat.

Sing me to sleep where camp fires blaze,
Boiling the water for *café-au-lait*;
Dreaming of home and nights up west,
Somebody's overseas [size?] boots on my chest.

Far, far from Ypres I long to be,
Where German snipers can't pot at me.
Think of me crouching where the worms creep,
Waiting for something to put me to sleep.

Sing me to sleep in some old shed,
Dozens of rat holes all round my head;
Stretched out upon my waterproof,
Dodging the raindrops through the roof.

Sing me to sleep where bombs explode
And shrapnel shells are *à la mode*.
Over the parapet helmets you'll find;
Corpses in front of me, corpses behind.

Far, far from starlights I long to be;
Public house bar lights I'd rather see.
Think of my curses, bitter and deep,
Writing these verses to help me to sleep.

~ · I WORE A TUNIC · ~

'A late-in-the-[First World] War song', comment John Brophy and Eric Partridge, 'and almost the only one which displays resentment against those who evaded military service.' The words parody a popular American song of 1915.

Tune: 'I Wore a Tulip'

> I wore a tunic, a lousy khaki tunic,
> And you wore civvy clothes.
> We fought and bled at Loos
> While you were home on the booze,
> The booze that no one here knows.
> Oh you were with the wenches
> While we were in the trenches,
> Facing an angry foe.
> Oh you were a-slacking
> While we were attacking
> The Jerry on the Menin Road.

Leicestershire Regiment group at Aldershot in the 1920s.
The author's father, George Palmer, is on the right of the seated row

ᢒᡕᢓ · OLD JOE WHIP · ᢒᡃᢒᢓ

The singer here, Jackie Booth of Stroud, Gloucestershire, was born in 1917, and served in the army in the 1930s. The song dates from the First World War, when it was known to American soldiers as 'The Brave Grenadier'. The tune comes from a song of 1911.

Tune: 'Casey Jones'

> Now listen all you good fellows here,
> I'll tell you the story of a bold bombardier.
> Now Old Joe Whip it was the brave man's name,
> And on a bombing stunt he won glorious fame:
> Kissed old Nobby at the doghouse door,
> Mounted the parapet at half past four,
> He mounted the parapet, his Mills bomb in his hand,
> And took a farewell trip into No Man's Land.
> (*Chorus*)
> *Old Joe Whip, mounted on the parapet,*
> *Old Joe Whip, a Mills bomb in his hand;*
> *Old Joe Whip, he stopped a blooming whizzbang,*
> *Now he's a bomber in the Promised Land.*
>
> Now Old Joe Whip, he had a dog named Ben,
> Had nine appetites, blooming near ten.
> He wouldn't eat meat, he wouldn't eat crusts,
> He'd eat rice pudding till he nearly bust.
>
> Now Old Joe Whip he went skating one day,
> Old Joe Whip went a-skating away;
> Old Joe Whip fell through a hole in the ice,
> Now he's a-skating out to Jesus Christ.

ᢒᡕᢓ · WHEN THIS POXY · ᢒᡃᢒᢓ
WAR IS OVER

'Are we weak and heavy-laden, Cumbered with a load of care?' asks the hymn, 'What a Friend we Have in Jesus'. Soldiers took it, and turned it into a heartfelt expression of longing for the end of war and release from the dangers and frustrations of army life. Like a number of First World War songs, this was also current during the Second. The version given here comes from George Hall, via his son, Gordon. George Hall of the Royal Sussex Regiment had a spell in the regimental prison at Chichester while awaiting demobilisation after the war, and was obliged to do cannon-ball drill, which explains the 'Pick it up' and 'Put it down' of the last verse.

Tune: 'What a Friend we Have in Jesus'

> When this poxy war is over no more soldiering for me.
> When I get my civvy clothes on, oh how happy I shall be.
> No more church parades on Sunday, no more begging for a pass.
> You can tell the sergeant-major to stick his passes up his arse.
>
> (*Repeat first two lines of first verse*)
> No more NCOs to curse me, no more rotten army stew.
> You can tell the old cook-sergeant to stick his stew right up his flue.
>
> (*Repeat first two lines of first verse*)
> No more sergeants bawling 'Pick it up' and 'Put it down'.
> If I meet the ugly bastard I'll kick his arse all round the town.

An officer is measured for his 'demob' suit at Olympia, London, at the end of the Second World War

(c) Between the Wars

GOODBYE, INDIA

Who fed me from a greasy pot,
And cursed me long in accents hot
When I said I liked his cooking not?
The Bobajee.

When sleep forsook my open eye,
Who was it sang sweet lullaby,
And brought me beer when I was dry?
The naik.

Who at reveille stroked my head
When sleeping on my trundle bed,
And tears of sweet affection shed?
The sergeant.

Who ran to help me when I fell,
And kissed the place to make it well,
Then consigned me to a place like hell?
The sergeant-major.

When fever or beer made me cry,
Who gazed upon my bloodshot eye,
And wept for fear that I might die?
The RAMC bloke.

Who, fed up with endless round,
Is getting daily bored and brown,
While I, thank God, am homeward bound?
Why, you are.

D Company, Wiltshire Regiment, marches past with new colours at Bangalore in India, 1938. Harold Wirdnam (see Introduction) is arrowed, third from the left

⸎ · SHAIBAH BLUES · ⸎

An RAF base was established at Shaibah on the Persian Gulf (now in Iraq) in the 1920s. The song, with its 'roll on' theme, could not fail to appeal to servicemen, and soldiers soon picked it up from airmen. It continued to be sung at least until the Second World War.

Tune: 'A Little Bit of Heaven'

> Oh a little piece of heaven fell from out the sky one day
> And it landed in the *bundu* not so very far away,
> And when the airforce saw it, oh, it looked so grim and bare,
> They said, 'That's what we're looking for, we'll build an airworks there.'
> So they sent out river gunboats, armoured cars and SHQs,
> And they put our squadron right in that *maknoon* blue.
> Now *peechi* I am waiting for that day that's far remote;
> Until that day you'll hear me say: 'Roll on that blinking boat.'
> I've got those Shaibah blues, Shaibah blues,
> Cheesed off and far from home.

⟨⟨ · HOLD YOUR ROW · ⟩⟩

Another RAF song, of similar vintage to 'Shaibah Blues', was also taken up by soldiers, who would have sung 'MPs' for 'SPs' and 'CB' for 'CC'. The theme of returning home is combined with those of the inconstancy of sweethearts left in England and the frustrations of venal relationships abroad.

Tune: 'Villikins'

> Way out in Iraq a fortnight I'd been
> When I got a message from my little queen,
> Saying how she'd got married a fortnight ago:
> 'Five years is a long time to wait, don't you know?'
> (*Chorus*)
> *Hold your row, wat'cher say,*
> *We can beat all the SPs who come down our way.*
>
> So I took to the bottle, I took to the glass,
> And I stuck to MacEwan's as long as it last,
> Till one night in Baghdad the cops picked up me,
> And the lousy old CO said: 'Fourteen CC.'
>
> Now Baghdad's a city of wonderful sights;
> The girls in the restaurants they all dress in tights,
> And they drink ginger ale while you pay for champagne,
> Then they say: 'Not tonight, dear, I'll see you again.'
>
> Fourteen more days and the boat will be here,
> Fourteen more days and we'll leave Basra Pier;
> And the finest of sights in the whole of Iran
> Is from the stern of a trooper that's not coming back.

⟨⟨ · THE ARTILLERY · ⟩⟩ ALPHABET

Lord Kitchener (verse three) died in 1916, so the song must date from before then. The words given here were popular among soldiers stationed in India in the 1930s.

A similar version, despite anachronistic references to horse-drawn guns, was sung during the Second World War by Canadian soldiers. (The Kitchener line, though, was replaced by: 'K is for keg what we all like a lot.') At the same time there was an adaptation for tanks, sung by the 10th (Border) Regiment, RAC, which included verses like this:

> M is for maintenance which we have to do,
> N is for nuts that we lose off the screw.
> O is for operator who gets on the set,
> And P is for panzers who we will beat yet.

Tune: 'The Artillery Alphabet'

> A stands for artillery, the pride of my heart.
> B stands for battery of which I'm a part.
> C stands for corrector, it gives us the fuse.
> D stands for dragropes we oft times do use.
> (*Chorus*)
> *Singing merry and merry and merry are we,*
> *We are the boys of the artillery.*
> *Blow high, blow low, wherever we go,*
> *We're all jolly fellows when out on a spree.*
>
> E stands for elevation, it guides the old shell.
> F stands for firing, we'll blow them to hell.
> G stands for gunner, he sticks and he sweats.
> H stands for horses, the drivers' best pets.
>
> I stands for infantry, we shoot over their heads.
> J stands for Jerry, he's sampled our lead.
> K stands for Kitchener, a jolly old sport.
> L stands for layer who's dropping them short.
>
> M stands for major, who's in command.
> N stands for nation, we'll make a firm stand.
> O stands for observer, he's never far out.
> P stands for pay sergeant, money for nowt.
>
> Q stands for quickness, we'll give it them hot.
> R stands for red tape of which there's a lot.
> S stands for signaller we can't do without.
> T stands for trumpeter who calls the boys out.
>
> U stands for unit of which we are proud.
> V stands for vehicle on which the lads crowd.
> W stands for wages, so damned hard to earn.
> X, Y, Z, we'll very soon learn.

Royal Horse Artillery Group in India, 1930s. John Gregson (middle row, third from left) had a fine repertoire of army songs (see Introduction)

❦ · MERRY BATTERY · ❧
BOYS

Whereas 'The Artillery Alphabet' to some extent reflects official attitudes ('we'll make a firm stand', 'we'll give it them hot'), this is very much an unofficial piece. It circulated among British soldiers in India (and no doubt elsewhere) in the 1930s.

Tune: based on 'Nick, Nack, Paddy Whack'

> Number one, number one,
> Scruffiest so-and-so on the gun.
> (*Chorus*)
> *With a rum tum tiddle um, tiddle um a day,*
> *Merry battery boys are we.*
>
> Number two, number two,
> He shoves a shell right up the flue.
>
> Number three, number three,
> Lays on an aiming point that he can't see.

Number four, number four,
He runs a shell right up the bloody bore.

Number five, number five,
He's more dead than he's a-bleeding live.

Number six, number six,
He gets the fuse bars in a right fix.

Number seven, number seven,
When he goes up he'll go to heaven.

Number eight, number eight,
He can laugh but he's a poor do at feight.

Number nine, number nine,
He scarpers off to the waggon lines.

Number ten, number ten,
Haven't had one since the Lord knows when.

· SIXTEEN ANNAS, · ONE RUPEE

The prime sentiment here seems to be Indian glee at the departure of the British, but the song was nevertheless sung by soldiers, like John Gregson, who served in the sub-continent between the wars. Another version, entitled 'Bombay Bibley', dates from the Second World War.

Sixteen annas, one rupee;
Seventeen annas, one buckshee.
Seven long years you've loved my daughter;
Now you go to Blighty, sahib.
May the boat that takes you over
Sink to the bottom of the *pani*, sahib.
(*Chorus*)
Oolen dal, oolen dal,
Aye ka bibi, aye ka bibi, bot a cha.

Sergeant-major, hollow ground razor,
Queen Victoria, very good man.
May the boat, *etc.*

An artilleryman of the First World War and his wife

ᶜᵍ · *ORDERLY MAN* · ᵔᵛ

A few days before reporting for national service in 1955 I took the trouble to go into the local reference library and read through *Queen's Regulations* and the *Manual of Military Law*. This gave me the distinction of immediate recognition on joining as a barrack-room lawyer – not, in the eyes of the authorities, a distinction.

The army's disciplinary machinery is formidable, and soldiers spend a good deal of time and effort in circumventing it. Here, after narrowly avoiding trouble a soldier bids a glad farewell to the army, on the expiration of his 'time'. An 'orderly man' was one whose name came up on a rota to perform certain tasks. The song was learnt in India between 1929 and 1936 by John Gregson, who commented: 'If you're doing seven years at two bob a day, you like to cock a snook.'

And now, kind gents, I've been called upon to sing you a little song,
So with your best attention, sure, it won't take very long.
I'll sing it out without a doubt and do the best I can,
And I'll tell you in the artillery how they do their orderly man.

Now it was 'Marching Orders', boys, when the corps went on the booze,
And I went sick next morning just to try to be excused.
The doctor only smiled at me and said: 'Look here, young man.
Get ready for marching orders, likewise do your orderly man.'

So I packs me pack upon me back and on parade I went.
I knew that I was dirty but I had to be content.
Sure, I was late as well as dirty and the officer he began:
'Seven days CB', said he to me, 'and do your orderly man.'

When he looked down me rifle, boys, it's then you should see the fun.
He said it was more like a chimmerly pot than it was like a gun.
He told the orderly sergeant for to parade me again at one,
But I had to fetch the dinner, boys, 'cause I was orderly man.

And now, me lads, my time is in and a soldier I'm no more;
I don't give a damn for the RFA or any other corps.
They can keep their kit and their six pound ten and do the best they can,
But they won't get me for another six to do their orderly man.

⤷ · *A SOLDIER'S* · ⤶
FAREWELL TO INDIA

The singer here, Harold Wirdnam, served in India with the Wiltshire Regiment from 1936 to 1944. The British Army undoubtedly fostered a sense of superiority towards 'lesser breeds without the law'. Homesickness also coloured soldiers' attitudes.

Tune: 'Underneath the Spreading Chestnut Tree'

> Land of pungent, sweltering heat,
> Land of dirty, sweaty feet,
> Where mosquitoes love to roam.
> I'll be glad when I get home.
>
> Land of cowdung, char and wads,
> Dirty, stinking, filthy bods.
> Land of things that bite at night,
> Mosquitoes' joy, bugs' delight.

Land of snakes and reptiles vile,
Land of rats up in the tiles,
Where the kitehawk is a cinch,
Where there's anything to pinch.

Land of lovely, sun-burnt maids,
Dusky skins which never fade.
Powder cannot make them white,
Even 'neath the electric light.

Land of sugar cane so sweet,
Dirty rivers, fly-blown meat.
Half-castes' heaven, soldiers' hell,
Land of black-necks, fare thee well.

Lord Linlithgow, Viceroy of India, watches (left) the Wiltshire Regiment paraded with its new colours and then takes his departure

⌦ · *CUT DOWN* · ⌫

As 'The Buck's Elegy', this song made its first appearance in the eighteenth century. As its many titles attest – they include 'Tarpaulin Jacket', 'St James' Hospital' and 'The Unfortunate Rake' – it was lately widely adapted and transmitted. A ritual funeral is usually present, though its subject (or object) varies: lad, lass, soldier, sailor, airman, gunner, marine. George Hewins (1878–1977), better known, perhaps, as 'The Dillen', remembered a scrap of the song which he had learned as a boy from one Gunner White, who had 'soldiered for the queen for twenty-two years and been discharged afore I was born'. Spike Mays, serving in the cavalry between the wars, had this verse:

> Wrap me up in my old stable jacket,
> And say a poor bastard lays low;
> And six Royal Dragoons they will carry me
> To the place where the best soldiers go.

The version given here comes from William Blackmore's scrapbook.

> One night as I wandered, my bed mate I followed.
> He was as drunk, yes, as drunk as could be.
> He asked for a candle to light him to bed,
> And early next morning he was found lying dead.
> (*Chorus*)
> *They played the pipes o'er him, they beat the drums melody [merrily],*
> *They played the dead march as they carried him along;*
> *And at his graveside three shots were fired o'er him,*
> *In memory of a soldier cut down in his prime.*
>
> Now on the street corner three flash girls were standing.
> Said one to the other in whispering tones:
> 'There goes the young soldier whose money we squandered,
> There goes the young soldier cut down in his prime.'
>
> There on his tombstone these few words were written:
> 'Now all you young soldiers, take warning from me.
> Don't go courting flash girls of the city;
> Flash girls of the city were the ruin of me.'

⟡ · THE CODFISH · ⟡

This crude and farcical story goes back at least to 1610, when it appeared in a collection of jokes and anecdotes published by Béroalde de Verville under the title of *Le Moyen de Parvenir*. The oldest version in English of the song occurs in an eighteenth-century manuscript as 'The Sea Crabb'. The version given here comes from George A. Bregenzer of Hayes, Middlesex, who learnt it from a friend serving with the RE territorials in the 1930s. Soldiers of the First World War sang something similar, entitled 'Tee, I, Ee, I, O'.

Oh there was a little man and he had a little horse,
And he saddled it and bridled it and cocked his leg across.
(*Chorus*)
With an aye tye aye, aye tye aye,
Aye tiddli aye tiddli aye tye aye.

Now he rode and he rode till he came to a brook,
And there he saw a fisherman a-fishing with a hook.

'Fisherman, fisherman, fisherman,' said he,
'Have you got a codfish to sell to me?'

'Oh yes, sir, yes, sir, I have two.
One for me and one for you.'

Now he got the codfish by the backbone,
Slung it across his shoulder and went off home.

Now when he got home he couldn't find a dish,
So he put it in the place where the old woman pissed.

Now all that night the old woman cried:
'There's a devil in the pisspot and I can see his eyes.'

So one got the shovel, the other got the broom,
Chased the poor cow's son all round the room.

Now they hit him in the head and they hit him in the side.
They hit him in the knackers till the poor sod died.

Now this is the end and there's never no more.
There's an apple up your gongapooch and you can have the core.

⤜ · CHILLI OF · ⤝
CHOWRINGHEE

The song reflects the malaise of the soldier briefly on leave but knowing that he will shortly be returning to action. The singer, Bill ('Pop') Hingston, was a medical orderly in the Devonshire Regiment from 1940 until 1952, serving mainly in India and Malaya. Chowringhee is the main street in Calcutta.

Tune: 'Lili Marlene'

> Walking down Chowringhee, dressed up to the nines,
> A white shirt and a bush hat and a badge that really shines.
> We know that the Nip is waiting in the *chung*,
> It won't be long till he hears our song.
> (*Chorus*)
> *My Chilli of Chowringhee, the blackest whore in town.*
>
> Resting in a *basha*, back behind the lines,
> Though we're resting now we'll soon be back for more.
> We know, *etc.*
>
> Dressed in boots and gaiters, blanket on the floor;
> Though we're dressed up now we will soon be back for more.
> We know there's a Nip a-waiting, *etc.*

⤜ · THE VALLEY OF · ⤝
JARAMA

For much of the Spanish Civil War (1936–39) a volunteer International Brigade fought on the side of the republican government against the fascist rebels. In 1937 fighting at the strategic Jarama Valley, just south of Madrid, went on for several months, and settled into a routine of trench warfare. The British Battalion, save for a brief respite on 1 May, was in the line for seventy-three days, and suffered heavy casualties.

The song was written by one of the men involved in the battle, Alex or Alec McDade, a former regular soldier from Glasgow. He took the tune (also well known during the Second World War) of a popular American song of the 1920s and 1930s, which in turn derived from a folk song entitled 'Bright Mohawk Valley'. McDade was killed at the Battle of Brunete in July 1938.

An anti-tank battery of the International Brigade which fought on the side of the republican government during the Spanish Civil War. Miles Tomalin is shown with a recorder, and Otto Estenson with a mandolin

His song is far removed from the cynicism of many soldiers' lyrics but it nevertheless expresses a certain war-weariness. It quickly became popular, and 'was sung in many versions, some ribald, some serious, and was taken over by all the nationalities' on the republican side. In amended form it became the anthem of the British Battalion, and is sung to this day at reunions and meetings. The original text is given here.

Tune: 'Red River Valley'

> There's a valley in Spain called Jarama,
> That's a place that we all know so well,
> For 'twas there that we wasted our manhood,
> And most of our old age as well.
>
> From this valley they tell us we're leaving,
> But don't hasten to bid us adieu,
> For e'en though we make our departure,
> We'll be back in an hour or two.
>
> Oh, we're proud of the British Battalion,
> And the marathon record it's made.
> Please do us this little favour
> And take this last word to Brigade.
>
> 'You will never be happy with strangers;
> They would not understand you as we,
> So remember the Jarama Valley
> And the old men who wait patiently.'

✍ · BLESS 'EM ALL · ✍

Overseas, and in peacetime, opportunities for promotion were few, and the petty restrictions of military life, many. For a man to board the homeward-bound troopship – in this case from India – at the end of his time was a dream come true.

A soldier reaching the end of his service often feels contempt mingled with pity for new recruits, especially when they are joining voluntarily. He also, at least in the lower ranks, has a bitter disdain for army life, softened only by exultant joy at his forthcoming liberation. The song's recurrent phrase, 'bless 'em all', was originally far stronger: 'rob 'em all', 'sod 'em all', and even 'fuck 'em all'.

Lewis Winstock's Chelsea Pensioners told him that the song was current in the army by the last decade of the nineteenth century. However, C. H. Ward-Jackson suggests that it, 'or rather a version not intended for publication', was written in 1916 by one Fred Godfrey, while he was a member of the Royal Naval Air Service. It seems more likely that Godfrey was merely writing down a song which was in circulation among servicemen in his day.

In turn, Jimmy Hughes and Frank Lake were responsible for an arrangement which became popular with civilians during the Blitz of September 1940 to May 1941, and remained so for the rest of the war. Soldiers sang both sanitised and scurrilous words, depending on the company in which they found themselves. There were versions for sailors, paratroops ('They say there's a Whitley just leaving Ringway'), bomber pilots ('There's many a Lancaster leaving the Ruhr') and coastal command flyers ('There's many a Hudson just leaving Norway'). Canadian soldiers sang it. So did Americans, and continued to do so through the Korean War and into the late 1950s at least. The version given here comes from the Stoke-on-Trent men who were prisoners-of-war in the 1940s.

There's many a troopship just leaving Bombay,
Bound for old Blighty's shore,
Heavily laden with time-expired men,
Bound for the land they adore.
There's many a corporal just serving his time,
And many a twat signing on.
They'll get no promotion this side of the ocean,
So cheer up, my lads, bless 'em all.

Boy bugler and drill sergeant
of the Queen's Westminster Volunteer Corps, 1897

(Chorus)
Bless 'em all, bless 'em all,
The long and the short and the tall.
Bless all the sergeants and WO Ones,
Bless all the corporals and their bastard sons,
For we're saying goodbye to them all,
As back to their billets they crawl.
You'll get no promotion this side of the ocean,
So cheer up, my lads, bless 'em all.

They say if you work hard you'll get better pay.
We've heard it all before.
Clean up your buttons and polish your boots,
Scrub out the barrack room floor.
There's many a swaddy has taken it in,
Hook, line and sinker and all.
You'll get, *etc.*

They say that the sergeant's a very nice bloke.
Oh what a tale to tell.
Ask him for leave on a Saturday night;
He'll pay your fare home as well.
There's many a swaddy has blighted his life,
Writing rude words on the wall.
You'll get, *etc.*

(Last Chorus)
Officers don't worry me,
Officers don't worry me.
Bell-bottomed trousers with stripes down the side,
Whacking great pockets with fuck-all inside.
We're saying goodbye, etc.

(d) The Second World War

A SOLDIER'S CATECHISM

What is your name? *A soldier.*

Who gave you that name? *The recruiting sergeant, when I received the enlisting shilling, whereby I was made a recruit of bullets, bayonets and sudden death.*

What did the recruiting sergeant promise for you? *That I should renounce all ideas of liberty and all such nonsense. That I should be well harassed with drill. That I should be stood up and shot at whenever called upon to do so.*

Rehearse the articles of your belief. *I believe in the colonel, most mighty, maker of sergeants and corporals, and his deputy, the major, an officer by commission, who rose by turn of promotion and has suffered the hardships of field service, marching, drill and fighting; he descended into trials; after the war he ascended into ease, and sitteth at the right hand of the colonel whence he shall come to separate the good from the bad. I believe in the adjutant, the punishment of the guardroom, the stoppage of my pay, the giving of defaulters, and the certainty of all these.*

How many commandments are there? *Ten, and they are:*
1. *Thou shalt have no other colonel but me.*
2. *On guard mounting thy braces shall not be wrongly crossed, nor shall thy rifle be unclean, neither thy hair uncut, nor thy safety catch up, for I shall punish these offenders unto the fourteenth day hereafter, and show mercy to them that keep my commandments.*
3. *Thou shalt not covet thy neighbour's badges, nor his marksman's badges, nor his cushy job, nor anything that is his.*
4. *Six days shalt thou labour and the seventh thou shalt clean up thy kit.*
5. *Thou shalt not walk with any of above your own rank.*
6. *Honour thy dining hall waiter, that he shall give unto thee buckshees.*
7. *Thou shalt kill all mosquitoes.*
8. *Thou shalt not drink thy comrade's beer, nor his char, nor any drink that is his.*
9. *Thou shalt not change thy socks or shirt or any clothing on Sundays.*
10. *Thou shalt not borrow thy comrade's holdall, nor his housewife, nor his blacking, nor his dubbin, nor his khaki drill, nor anything that is his for kit inspection.*

ᘓᘓ · *THE DIGGER'S SONG* · ᘓᘓ

The front-line soldier's contempt for those in 'soft' positions made this song popular with British, American and Australian troops in two World Wars. Indeed, this version seems to amalgamate details from the First World War such as the reference to 'whizzbangs' with those from the Second (Lord Gort, a highly decorated and distinguished soldier of the First World War was Chief of the Imperial General Staff from 1939 to 1940).

One version changes the first couplet of verse two to:

> The digger then shot him a murderous look.
> He said, 'I'm just back from that place called Tobruk.'

Another, to the tune of 'The Mountains of Mourne', and without a chorus, is very uninhibited in its language. The third verse, for example, runs:

> The digger jumped up with a murderous glance,
> Said, 'Fuck you, I just came from the trenches in France,
> Where fighting was plenty and cunt was for few,
> And brave men were dying for shitbags like you.'

A third was learned by Pete Seeger while serving with the American Army in the South Pacific, late in the war.

Tune: 'Villikins'

> He came up to London and straightway he strode
> To the army headquarters in Horseferry Road,
> To see all the bludgers who dodge all the strafe
> By getting soft jobs on the headquarters staff.
> (*Chorus*)
> *Dinky-die, dinky-die,*
> *I am an old digger and can't tell a lie.*

> A lousy lance-corporal said, 'Pardon me, please.
> There's blood on your tunic, there's mud on your sleeve.
> You look so disgraceful that people will laugh,'
> Said the lousy lance-corporal on the headquarters staff.

> The digger then shot him a murderous glance;
> He said, 'I'm just back from the shambles in France,
> Where the whizzbangs are flying and comforts are few,
> And brave men are dying for bastards like you.

'We're shelled on the left and we're shelled on the right.
We're bombed all the day and we're bombed all the night.
If something don't happen, and that pretty soon,
There'll be nobody left in the bloody platoon.'

The story was brought to the ears of Lord Gort,
Who gave the whole matter a great deal of thought,
Then awarded that digger a VC and two bars
For giving that corporal a kick in the arse.

· IN BLOODY ORKNEY ·

The Orkney Islands, with their tiny population, were garrisoned during the Second World War by a huge force of servicemen. On the single island of Hoy, for example, there were 30,000 sailors. The men had very little to do when they were off duty, and their boredom and disgust were expressed in a song written by Captain Hamish Blair. Its text was adapted to suit various RAF stations, including Shrimpton-Bassett in Wiltshire. The Ayrshire Yeomanry, having been stationed in Orkney, took the song on moving to Caithness in 1941 and used it as the basis for 'Oh! Fucking Halkirk'. Captain Blair's original is still on sale in Kirkwall at the offices of *The Orcadian* in the form of a single sheet on which are added two contemporary ripostes, one of which runs:

> The bloody Sassenachs have come
> With bugle call and tuck o' drum,
> With smell of beer and Army rum,
> The cheeky sods.
> What right have they to criticise
> Who blow their trumpets to the skies,
> But all our folk and homes despise,
> The bloody clods.
>
> We love the winds, we like the rains,
> We do have kerbs and likewise drains,
> We have no trams or railway trains,
> But ships and luggers.
> O could we hear the farewell knell
> Of old St Magnus' Church's bell,
> To send them all to bloody hell,
> The cocky buggers.

Captain Blair, who was no Sassenach if his name is anything to go by, specified no tune, so soldiers no doubt fitted their own.

Tune: 'Early in the Morning' or 'Baa, Baa, Black Sheep'

> This bloody town's a bloody cuss,
> No bloody trains, no bloody bus;
> And no one cares for bloody us
> In bloody Orkney.

The following three photographs show scenes from the daily life of anti-aircraft gunners stationed on Orkney, June 1944

The bloody roads are bloody bad,
The bloody folks are bloody bad;
They make the brightest bloody sad
In bloody Orkney.

All bloody cloud, all bloody rain,
No bloody kerbs, no bloody drains;
The council's got no bloody brains,
In bloody Orkney.

The bloody flicks are bloody old,
The bloody seats are bloody cold;
You can't get in for bloody gold,
In bloody Orkney.

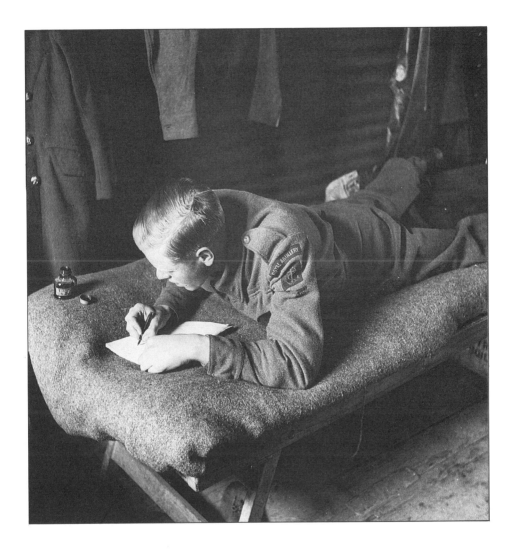

The bloody dances make you smile,
The bloody band is bloody vile;
It only cramps your bloody style,
In bloody Orkney.

No bloody sport, no bloody games,
No bloody fun; the bloody dames
Won't even give their bloody names,
In bloody Orkney.

There's nothing greets your bloody eye
But bloody sea and bloody sky.
'Roll on demob,' we bloody cry,
In bloody Orkney.

ᥴᥣᥓ · THE ROYAL · ᥘᥩ ARTILLERY

Members of the rank and file frequently hold adverse opinions of the competence of those in command. This song of the Second World War (the use of the word 'show' for an action or indeed a war being absolutely typical of the time) recalls 'Our Essex Camp' from the First, and employs the same tune.

Tune: 'Down Home in Tennessee'

I enlisted as a gunner
In the King's RA
For four and nine a day
Which wasn't too bad pay,
But it's all 'Jump to it', 'Run there',
And 'Man that gun there',
All the lousy day;
And each evening
In the wet canteen
We sing this roundelay:

We are tired hands,
Too tired even to stand.
Our sergeant-major
He's a regular twit you see,
And our officers too
Are the worst I ever knew.
Talk about leaders,
They ought to be in feeders.
Oh what shall we do?
We'll offer up our thanks.
Thank heaven we've got the tanks,
The WRAAFs and Air Force too;
And when this show is over
I'll beat it hotfoot back to Dover
And departee gay and hearty
To my home in Battersea.

ᏣᏋ · *SOLDIER AND SAILOR* · ᏋᏉ

Over a long period of time, and in many different versions, this was widely popular in all three services as well as outside them. Cecil Sharp had a version learned from a singer born in 1779, and thought that the song descended from 'The Mare and the Foal', a dialogue excoriating dishonest tradesmen, but the reverse may be the case. A street ballad text, issued between 1863 and 1885 under the title of 'The Soldier & The Sailor', explicitly brings together military and civilian abuse:

> There's our Buttys, and our Baileys, and our Dogges also,
> There's our corporals and our managers as you very well do know,
> They do line their backs well by the labouring poor,
> May the Devil double tribble damn them: said the soldier, 'Amen'.

One veteran of the Boer War remembered a verse sung at that time which is remarkably similar to the last verse of version A here:

> It's captains and colonels and lieutenants, too,
> Sergeants, colour-sergeants and corporals likewise;
> With their hands in their pockets they rob us poor men.
> May the Lord damn and blast them. Says the soldier, 'Amen'.

During the Second World War the Canadian forces had their own versions. One of these, remarkably, expressed the woman's viewpoint:

> 'The first thing we'll ask for, we'll ask for some men,
> And may we have one more for every good Wren;
> And if we get one more may we also get ten,
> Take the whole ruddy convoy.' Said the XO [Executive Officer], 'Amen'.

The song has continued to circulate to the present day.

ᏣᏋᏉ

A.

A soldier and a sailor went a-walking one day.
Said the sailor to the soldier: 'Let's kneel down and pray;
And if we say one prayer may we also say ten.
May we have a Church of England.' Said the soldier, 'Amen'.

'The first thing we'll pray for, we'll pray for our queen.
Long may she live and long may she reign;
And if she has one kid may she also have ten.
May she have a bloody regiment.' Said the soldier, 'Amen'.

'And the next thing we'll pray for, we'll pray for our beer.
Lordy, when we get it we'll give it a cheer;
And if we have one pint may we also get ten.
May we have a bloody brewery.' Said the soldier, 'Amen'.

'The next thing we'll pray for, we'll pray for our pay.
Lordy, when we get it we'll shout out "Hooray";
And if we get one pound may we also get ten.
May we have the Bank of England.' Said the soldier, 'Amen'.

'And the next thing we'll pray for, we'll pray for our cunt.
Glory, when we get it we'll shout and we'll grunt;
And if we have one bint, may we also have ten.
May we have a bloody brothel.' Said the soldier, 'Amen'.

'The officers and sergeants and sergeant-majors, too,
Rotten lot of bastards with fuck all to do;
Hands in their pockets to shout at their men.
May the Lordy double fuck them.' Said the soldier, 'Amen'.

B.
Said the matlow to the swaddie, 'Let's all pray for beer.
Glory hallelujah, we'll raise one big cheer;
And if we sink one pint may we also sink ten.
May we own a fucking brewery.' Said the swaddie, 'Amen'.

Said the swaddie to the matlow, 'Let us pray for our king.
Glory in excelsis, his praises we'll sing;
And if he has one gun, a Browning or a Bren,
May he soon own a fucking arsenal.' Said the matlow, 'Amen'.

Said the matlow to the swaddie, 'Let us pray for a bint.
Glory, roll on payday, even purser is skint;
A NAAFI girl, an AT, a fat WAAF or a Wren,
May she not be a fucking mirage.' Said the swaddie, 'Amen'.

Said the swaddie to the matlow, 'Let us all pray for leave.
Glory, metal polish, we'll blanco and heave
On the lead, on the floor, on Saida's* front door,
Till we both get back to fucking Blighty, then we'll both pray no more.'
Amen, Amen, Amen.

* Queen to King Farouk of Egypt.

ᘓᕽᕽ · *HOW DID I EVER* · ᕽᕽᘓ
BECOME A CORPORAL?

A Second World War song showing the typically levelling attitude of the rank and file.

How did I ever become a corporal?
How did I get these stripes?
It's a mystery, I declare.
Did I get them on the square,
Or when the company quartermaster-sergeant wasn't there?
In the Boys' Brigade I was never on parade,
And I always liked my morning cup of tea.
How did I ever become a corporal?
It's a bloomin' mystery.

ᘓᕽᕽ · *ROLL ME OVER* · ᕽᕽᘓ

The inexorable progression, subject only to the exigencies of the internal rhyme in the first line of each verse, provides the fascination of this song. Again, some Chelsea Pensioners interviewed by Lewis Winstock suggested that it was current by the last decade of the nineteenth century. During the Second World War a version was sung by Canadian servicemen. In Britain it was known to men, women and children, with many variations in rhyme, length and coarseness. Gordon Hall, the singer of the version given here, varies the phrase 'in the clover' to 'British soldier', 'Yankee soldier', 'Polish soldier', 'Canadian soldier' or 'Free French soldier'.

Now this is number one and the fun has just begun.
(Chorus)
Roll me over, lay me down, and do it again.
Roll me over in the clover,
Roll me over, lay me down, and do it again.

Now this is number two and his hand is on my shoe.

Now this is number three and his hand is on my knee.

Now this is number four and we're rolling on the floor.

Now this is number five and he's tickling my thighs.

Now this is number six and I like his artful tricks.

Now this is number seven and I'm on my way to heaven.

Now this is number eight and I'm getting in a state.

Now this is number nine and the quads are doing fine.

Now this is number ten and he's at it once again.

Now this is number eleven and another trip to heaven.

Now this is number twelve, and he said, 'Just help yourself.'

· LULU ·

In many soldiers' songs, it cannot be denied, women are seen as the classic sex objects of feminist demonology. The language employed is often crude, though here there is a strange mixture of the coarse and the euphemistic. 'Lulu' was known during the Second World War to American, Canadian and British servicemen.

Lulu was my sweetheart, Lulu was so cute.
The first time that I met her she was a prostitute.
(*Chorus*)
Oh blimey she was a lulu, every inch a lulu,
Lulu, that little girl of mine.

I took her to the seaside to teach her how to swim,
And every time I ducked her head she swore I touched her quim.

I wish I was a diamond ring upon my Lulu's hand,
And every time she wiped her arse I'd see the promised land.

I wish I was a pisspot under Lulu's bed,
And every time she had a piss I'd see her maidenhead.

CE · HOW ASHAMED · SD
I WAS

The enumeration in song of parts of the female body progressively attained during an amorous encounter has an apparently perennial fascination. It dates back to at least 1608, and Thomas Heywood's play, *The Rape of Lucrece*, which includes a catch beginning (somewhat tastelessly, one might think):

> Did he take fair Lucrece by the toe, man? Toe, man? Ay, man.
> Ha ha ha ha ha, man.
> And further did he strive to go, man? Go, man? Ay, man.
> Ha ha ha ha, man, fa derry down, ha fa derry dino.

In the Second World War song there is a curious contradiction between the implied reticence of the oft-repeated 'how ashamed I was' and the shameless language and behaviour of the protagonists. Despite its subject matter the song is extraordinarily anti-erotic, and ends decidedly in a whimper rather than a bang. (Or rather, the bang ends in a whimper.) A Canadian version attempts to revive masculine pride by adding a final verse:

> And when the baby came
> The bastard had no name.

A re-write, also from Canada, deals with the tribulations of a recruit to the WAAFs, though completely without sexual reference.

> I touched her on the knee, ⎫ *bis*
> *How ashamed I was.* ⎭
> I touched her on the knee.
> She said, 'You're rather free.'
> (*Chorus*)
> *Oh gawd blimey how ashamed I was.*
>
> I touched her on the thigh.
> She said, 'You're getting high.'
>
> I touched her on the twat.
> She said, 'You're rather hot.'

I put the bugger in.
She said, 'It's rather thin.'

I pulled the bugger out.
She gave it such a clout.

I laid it on the grass.
She said, 'You'd better put it up your arse.'

· WATCH AND CHAIN · SONG

The opening verse leads us to expect a classic folk song, but instead we have an exercise of the kind much loved by schoolchildren and soldiers in the avoidance of rude words which seem inexorably destined to follow the rhyming pattern. The song was learnt during the Second World War but was probably in circulation before it.

As I was out walking one morning in May
I met a fair maiden so charming and gay.
I said: 'Pretty maiden, may I walk with you?'
She gave her consent so I walked with her too.

We walked and we walked till we came to a brook.
I said: 'Pretty maiden, may I have a swim?'
I swam and I swam till I grew very sick,
And when I came out she examined my

Gold watch and chain which I'd left in her care;
The face was all broken, no fingers were there.
She took me to a house which had trees in the front,
She took me upstairs and she showed me her

Union Jack which was red, white and blue.
I saw something else but I'm not telling you.

· THE ARMY DANCE ·

Some women's alleged sexual insatiability and the enormity of their sexual apparatus are frequent subjects for men's comments. This song has both army and navy versions, which probably derive from the eighteenth-century 'Fire Ship', which warns, albeit in jocular manner, about venereal disease. This was the first song heard in the wet canteen by Frank Richards after joining the army at Wrexham in 1901.

Tune: 'Come, Landlord, Fill the Flowing Bowl' or 'Dark and Roving Eye'

First there came the general's wife,
And she was dressed in grey, sir;
And in her quite enormous quim
She had a brewer's dray, sir.
(Chorus)
She had those dark and dreamy eyes,
And she sang a song of love, sir.
She was one of those black-eyed bints,
She was one of the brigade.

Next there came the colonel's wife,
And she was dressed in red, sir;
And in her quite enormous quim
She had a feather bed, sir.

Next there came the sergeant's wife,
And she was dressed in black, sir;
And in her quite enormous quim
She had a chimney stack, sir.

Next there came the corporal's wife,
And she was dressed in brown, sir;
And in her quite enormous quim
She had all Tidworth town, sir.

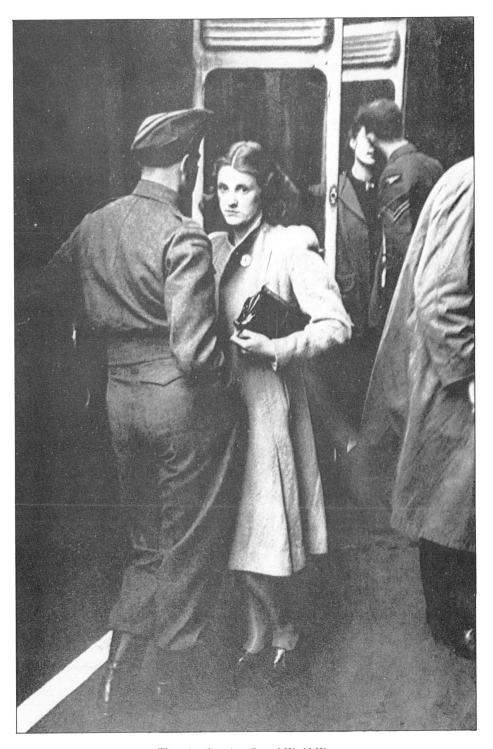

The pain of parting, Second World War

ᕳᕬᕲ · *DIED FOR LOVE* · ᕬᕲᕲ

It is undeniable that servicemen enjoy crude songs, but they also have a strong liking for the sentimental. John Gregson learnt a version of this song in India in the 1930s, and the Stoke prisoners-of-war remembered another which they had heard sung by the pot bank girls of the Potteries at the same period. During the Second World War there were army, navy and air force versions. The one given here is sung by Gordon Hall, whose brother, Lionel, learnt it while stationed as a soldier in the Faeroe Islands from 1941 to 1943.

A miner coming home one night
Found his house without a light;
And so he went upstairs to bed,
And then a thought entered his head.

He went into his daughter's room,
And found her hanging from a beam.
He took a knife and cut her down,
And in her hand this note he found.

'I had a lover and I loved him,
I loved him really fond and true,
Until he ran away and left me
To face this barren world alone.

'My brothers they have turned against me,
My sisters they have done the same;
But still my darling mother loves me.
My father's head is bent in shame.

'So, Mother, should you see my lover,
Greet him with a tender smile.
Although he ran away and left me
He's still the father of my child.

'My clothes are all in rags and tatters,
Just for to keep my baby warm.
Sleep on, sleep on, my blue-eyed treasure,
For soon your mammy will be gone.

'My love is for a bold marine.
I always, always think of him,
And though he's far across the sea
He never, never thinks of me.

'So all good maidens, bear in mind
A good man's love is hard to find.
Dig my grave both wide and deep,
And lay my weary bones to sleep.'

They dug her grave both wide and deep,
And laid white lilies at her feet;
And on her breast a turtle dove
To show the world she died for love.

A portrait sent home
by Harold Wirdnam of the Wiltshire Regiment

Good news from home

ᘓᘓᘓ · THE MERRY MONTH · ᘓᘓᘓ
OF MAY

Laughter, even on solemn occasions, can relieve tension or dispel gloom. Medical students, for example, are notorious for their practical jokes and jolly songs in connection with the dissection of corpses. Such behaviour is clearly a defence mechanism, which also works with other professions.

This song's light-hearted treatment of a paratrooper's departure and death is a case in point. It originally concerned a simple trooper, so the adaptation to paratrooper was easy. In this form it dates from the Second World War.

On her leg she wears a silken garter,
She wears it in the springtime, in the merry month of May,
And if you ask her why the hell she wears it,
She wears it for a paratrooper far, far away.
Far away, far away,
She wears it for a paratrooper who is far, far away.

Around the park she wheels a perambulator,
She wheels it in the springtime, in the merry month of May,
And if you ask her why the hell she wheels it,
She wheels it for a paratrooper far, far away.
Etc.

Behind the door her father keeps a shotgun,
He keeps it in the springtime, in the merry month of May,
And if you ask him why the hell he keeps it,
He keeps it for a paratrooper who is far, far away.
Etc.

The paratrooper went to join his unit,
He joined it in the springtime, in the merry month of May,
And if you ask him why the hell he joined it,
He joined it be very, very far, far away.
Etc.

In her hand she holds a bunch of daisies,
She holds them in the springtime, in the merry month of May,
And if you ask her why the hell she holds them,
She holds them for a paratrooper six feet down.
Etc.

✍ · PARATROOPER'S · ✎ SONG

It is interesting to see how quickly songs emerged to reflect the innovatory techniques of paratroopers, and the hazards they faced. The bravado shown here is clearly a defence mechanism.

Tune: 'John Brown's Body'

> I'd like to find the sergeant who forgot to hook me up (*ter*),
> (*Chorus*)
> *For I ain't going to jump no more.*
> *Glory, glory, what a hell of a way to die* (*ter*),
> *I ain't going to jump no more.*
>
> I'd like to find the WAAF that put a blanket in my 'chute.
>
> I'd like to find the pilot who forgot to throttle back.
>
> I landed on the tarmac like a gob of strawberry jam.
>
> They put me in a box that measured six by four by two.

✍ · THIS OLD COAT OF · ✎ MINE

Beery sing-songs known as 'sods' operas' went on in all three services. In the army these were held for the lower ranks in the wet canteen or barrack room, for sergeants in their mess. One soldier's account of the performances of 'This Old Coat' could be paralleled from both navy and air force:

> [It] was delivered by a singer who gradually stripped off as he sang one verse about each article of clothing and the scenes it had witnessed. When he threw off his pants he was seized by his drunken mates and subjected to various indignities.

The song has been reported from the 1920s and 1930s as well as from the Second World War, but is undoubtedly much older still. It may have originated with the sailors of the Atlantic packet ships of the mid-nineteenth century; certainly, one version was quoted in a midshipman's logbook of 1860.

> Oh this old hat of mine, the inside is quite new,
> The outside has seen some very fine weather,
> So I throw this hat of mine to the ocean wild and wide.
> (*Chorus*)
> *Roll on the boat that takes me home.*

Repeat in turn with 'coat', 'shirt', 'these old shoes', 'these old pants', *etc.*

· ON THE MOVE ·

'The boat for Blighty' recurs in this song, which originated in the Middle East during the 1940s. The tune seems to be a distant relative of 'Bless 'em All'.

> Pack the equipment all ready for shipment,
> We're on the move again;
> Forget your dejection and do an inspection
> On every aeroplane.
>
> I wonder where we're moving to.
> We don't know. Who does? Do you?
> However, we'll know when we get there,
> And rumours of Blighty are in the air.
>
> We used to be in India
> Till we went to Singapore,
> Then we moved across to Aden
> When the Eyeties joined the war.
>
> Later we went to Egypt,
> And after that to Greece;
> But roll on that boat for Blighty
> And a spot of blooming peace.

ᘓᑏᑏ · THE BALLAD OF WADI · ᑏᑏᘓ MAKTILLA

Hamish Henderson points out that this song of his, which dates from 1940, 'describes a somewhat abortive raid by the 2nd Camerons on an Italian outpost about twelve miles east of Sidi Barrani'. *Cabar Feidh* ('the deer's antlers') was the war cry of the Mackenzies and later of the Seaforth Highlanders. Henderson believes that there must have been some Seaforths seconded to the Cameron battalion which fought at Maktilla. (Both Seaforths and Camerons are now amalgamated into the Queen's Own Highlanders.) The Italian cry of 'Bruno' might be the name of a local commander; it was also that of one of Mussolini's sons. 'Hackit-skin' is Scots for chopped-up skin.

Tune: 'Villikins'

Now here is my story, it happened one night,
How the Seventy-Ninth they went into a fight.
They were carried in lorries over bump, rock and cranny –
Many arses were sore on that road to Barrani,
(*Chorus*)
What the hell's all the fuss?
Oh wouldn't you, wouldn't you like to be us?

Then we hoofed it along, lads, to Musso's armed villa –
A stronghold it was, and named Wadi Maktilla.
We tiptoed along as we came near our mark;
Not a sound could be heard, all was silent and dark.

Then suddenly the Eyeties let go all they had;
It's a bloody good job that their aiming was bad.
We got down on the ground and we lay as if dead,
While the shells and the whizzbangs flew over our head.

Many lads prayed to heavens which before they'd forsaken,
And they thought they'd eaten their last of tinned bacon;
But the Eyeties felt worse as they lay in their sangars,
And their guns roared in fear, for it wasn't in anger.

There were Libyans against us, they were filthy and black,
But we yelled *Cabar Feidh!* as we pressed the attack.
Then the Wops shouted 'Bruno' on whom they were nuts,
But they got for their pains our cold steel in their guts.

Now most of the Camerons, there isn't a doubt,
Got corns on their knees from this crawling about;
But the blokes that lay flat brought us many a grin,
For most of their bellies were all hackit-skin.

When at last we emerged from that unhealthy zone,
We got in the trucks and we headed for home.
You can say what you like, you have plenty of scope,
Do you think we enjoyed it? My Christ! What a hope!

· THE SONG OF THE 258 · GENERAL TRANSPORT

During the desert war of 1940–1 in North Africa, transport convoys were regularly bombed and strafed by Italian planes. Mersa Matruh is mentioned in several songs (see, for example, page 170); Jarabub is an oasis to the west of it.

Tune: 'Villikins'

Now the 258 General Transport are out here;
They dash up and down the desert in top gear.
They have many punctures and back axles cracked,
But they're quickly repaired – that's the best of the macs.
Toodle eh, toodle eh,
But they're quickly repaired – that's the best of the macs.

One day in the desert while having some lunch
The sergeant said, 'Now, boys, I've got a hunch.
Supposing we grease all our nipples today
It will help us run faster when we run away.'

One day while out on the Jarabub run
Three Eyeties dived at us from out of the sun.
Their bullets they whistled and whizzed through the air,
But where those bullets went there was nobody there.

Now when we get back home in the pubs we will dive.
We'll tell them we're lucky to get back alive;
We'll talk of the things that we once used to do,
Such as pinching the tinned fruit from Mersa Matruh.

Rex Gregson of the Royal Signals
and (opposite) a musical comrade, Sid Walker, in North Africa

·MY LITTLE DUGOUT·
IN THE SAND

The Eighth Army's westward progress across North Africa reached Tripoli in January 1942, which explains the song's comment that 'the Western Desert ain't western any more'. The singer, Rex Gregson, served in North Africa with the Royal Signals. Another version, beginning 'I'm a lousy, greasy gunner' was sung by members of the Northumberland Fusiliers.

Tune: 'I'm an Old Cowhand'

'I'm a signalman stationed in Matruh;
I've got a little dugout in the sand.
The flies gather round me as I settle down to rest,
In my flea-bound, bug-bound dugout in Matruh.
(*Chorus*)
The door is non-existent, the windows four by two,
The sandbags let the rain and blizzard through,
But I'm happy as the band in this land of shit and sand,
In my flea-bound, bug-bound dugout in Matruh.

The desert's littered over with bully and meat roll,
Jam and marmalade we never see.
I wish I had my sweetie to sit upon my knee,
I'd tell her all the troubles I've been through
In my *etc.*

So I'm saying goodbye to the desert,
Hang my beret on a nail behind the door.
Hand me down my civvy suit, sergeant-major,
'Cause the Western Desert ain't western any more.

⚜ · *NEVER GO TO MERSA* · ⚜

Mersa (or Marsa) Matruh is a town in Egypt which was repeatedly fought over during the desert campaigns of the Second World War. The song, which may have other verses which have not yet come to light, reflects the feelings of members of the British garrison after the German Army had finally been driven out.

Tune: 'John Brown's Body'

We eat the flies, we eat the shit, we eat the burning sand.
Our bones are getting brittle and our faces getting tanned.
Why the hell they keep us here we'll never understand,
But we'll sing our blues away.
(*Chorus*)
Never, never go to Mersa; never, never go to Mersa;
Never, never go to Mersa, it's a lousy place to stay.

Every Sunday morning we march across the sand;
The padre stands before us with his Bible in his hand.
We give our thanks to God and join his happy band
As we sing our blues away.

⚜ · *SEVEN YEARS* · ⚜
IN THE SAND

According to Ewan MacColl, this was the unofficial anthem of every unit which served in the Middle East during the Second World War, and was exceeded in popularity only by 'King Farouk'. The version given here may be a fragment from a longer text.

(*Chorus*)
Seven years in the sand seems a long time somehow.
Never mind, tosh, you'll soon be dead, a hundred years from now.

The pay is low, the grub is rank, you get jankers now and then.
You're fed almost entirely on the produce of the hen.

ᴄᴈ · *FUCKING TOBRUK* · ᴈᴅ

Like Mersa Matruh, Tobruk (in Libya) changed hands several times during the Second World War, before being definitively taken by the British in November 1942. The garrison, mainly consisting of Australians of the 9th Division, was under siege for a couple of months in 1941. During this time one of the soldiers wrote the song, or rather adapted it from 'Fucking Halkirk' or 'Bloody Orkney' (page 148).

Tune: 'Early in the Morning' or 'Baa, Baa, Black Sheep'

All fucking fleas, no fucking beer,
No fucking booze since we've been here;
And will it come? No fucking fear,
In fucking Tobruk.

The fucking rumours make me smile.
The fucking wogs are fucking vile.
The fucking pommies cramp your style
In fucking Tobruk.

All fucking dust, no fucking rain,
All fucking fighting since we came;
The army's just a fucking shame
In fucking Tobruk.

The bully makes me fucking wild,
I'd nearly eat a fucking child;
The salt water makes me fucking riled
In fucking Tobruk.

Air raids all day and fucking night,
Huns striving with all fucking might;
They give us all a fucking fright
In fucking Tobruk.

Best fucking place is fucking bed
With blanket over fucking head,
And then they think you're fucking dead
In fucking Tobruk.

ᘓ · *SHARI WAG* · ᘔ
EL BURKA

Soldiers, deprived of female companionship for long periods, and often facing an uncertain future, were regular customers of whorehouses. The 'flash girls' and their ravages of 'Cut Down' (page 138) here give way to a cruder and lighter warning in a song which dates from the Second World War. In Cairo the Wagh el Birket (Pond Street) was known to English-speakers as 'the Berka'. The long narrow street was full of booths with prostitutes, peepshows and pornographic cabarets. It was bounded by round white signs with a black cross, signifying that it was out of bounds to all ranks, but the prohibition was widely ignored by men of the Eighth Army who were on leave in the city.

Tune: 'Onward, Christian Soldiers'

There is a street in Cairo, full of sin and shame.
Shari Wag El Burka is the bastard's name.
(*Chorus*)
Russian, Greek and French bints all around I see,
Shouting out: 'You stupid prick, abide with me.'

Two or three weeks later when I see my dick,
Swiftly pack my small kit and fall in with the sick.

Five or six months later, free from sin and shame,
Back to the El Burka, just for fun and games.

· THE STREETS OF · MINTURNO

The Italian town of Minturno is at the mouth of the River Garigliano, eighteen miles west of Cassino. It was captured by the British in January 1944.

Now there is blood on the streets of Minturno,
It's the blood of the brave and the few;
The division that went into battle,
They do a job that no other can do.

Now the Yanks they said they couldn't cross the river,
They said it just couldn't be done;
And to prove what they thought of our chances
They were betting us twenty to one.

But they didn't know the old 5th Division;
When there were a job to be done
There weren't nothing on earth that could stop us,
Not even the square-headed Hun.

So forward we went into battle,
Not a man thought of death;
All grim and looking determined,
But in their hearts they were saying a prayer.

Yet they thought of their wives and their mothers,
They thought of their loved ones who'd yearned,
For they knew when they crossed over the river
There was many who'd never return.

Yes, there is blood on the streets of Minturno,
It's the blood of the brave and the few.
May their souls live in glory for ever,
And their hearts live in heaven above.

∽ · THE HIGHLAND · ∿ DIVISION'S FAREWELL TO SICILY

Hamish Henderson volunteered for the army at the beginning of the Second World War, but was turned down because of bad eyesight. A little later, though, he was conscripted into the Pioneer Corps, then transferred because of his knowledge of languages to the Intelligence Corps. As an intelligence officer he served with the 51st Highland Division through Eygpt, Libya, Tunisia, and then the invasions of Sicily and the mainland of Italy.

He was inspired to write what Norman Buchan has called 'the best song to come out of World War II' by the playing of a pipe band in Linguaglossa, a village on the slopes of Mount Etna, and the sight of exhausted soldiers relaxing. He had in mind a tune composed by Pipe-Major Robertson of Banff, and drew on the verbal idiom of the bothy songs of north-east Scotland. Some of the words used have these meanings in standard English: 'pipie', pipe-major; 'fey', in a strange state; 'unco', odd; 'chaulmers', bedrooms, especially for farm servants; 'eerie', ghost-like; 'shaw', wood; 'kyles', straits; 'smoor', smother; 'ava', at all; 'beezed', polished; 'shieling', hut; 'shebeens', drinking dens; 'bothies', stone outhouses used to accommodate farm servants.

Tune: 'Farewell to the Creeks'

> The pipie is dozie, the pipie is fey,
> He winna come roon for his vino the day.
> The sky ower Messina is unco an' grey
> And a' the bricht chaulmers are eerie.
> (*First chorus*)
> *Then fare well ye banks o' Sicily,*
> *Fare ye well, ye valley an' shaw.*
> *There's nae Jock will mourn the kyles o' ye,*
> *Puir bliddy bastards are weary.*
> *And fare well ye banks o' Sicily,*
> *Fare ye weel ye valley an' shaw.*
> *There's nae hame can smoor the wiles o' ye,*
> *Puir bliddy bastards are weary.*

> Then doon the stair and line the waterside,
> Wait your turn, the ferry's awa.
> Then doon the stair and line the waterside,
> A' the bricht chaulmers are eerie.

*Troops of the Highland Division wading ashore during the Allied landings
on Sicily, July 1943*

The drummie is polisht, the drummie is braw,
He cannae be seen for his webbin' ava.
He's beezed himsel up for a photo an' a'
Tae leave wi' his Lola, his dearie.
(*Second chorus*)
Then fare ye well ye dives o' Sicily,
Fare ye well ye shieling an' ha';
And fare ye well ye byres and bothies
Where kind signorinas were cheerie.
And fare ye weel ye dives o' Sicily,
Fare ye weel ye shieling an' ha'.
We'll a' mind shebeens and bothies
Whaur Jock made a date wi' his dearie.

Then tune the pipes and drub the tenor drum,
Leave your kit this side o' the wa';
Then tune the pipes and drub the tenor drum,
A' the bricht chaulmers are eerie.

On the Anzio beachhead, March 1944. Hamish Henderson, Intelligence Officer, 1st British Division (and songwriter – see pp. 174) is shown in the centre. With him (from left to right) are Pipe-major Boyd (6th Gordons), Pipe-major McConnachie (2nd Royal Scots), Drum-major Watson and Pipe-major Riach (both 6th Seaforths). The pipers were employed on the beachhead as stretcher-bearers

৫৬ · BALLAD OF ANZIO · ৩৩

During the Second World War the liberation of Italy – and indeed of western Europe – started with Allied landings on Sicily in July 1943. Progress up the mainland peninsula proved very difficult, and was assisted by further sea-borne assaults at Salerno (September 1943) and Anzio, some thirty-five miles south of Rome (January 1944). Both of these involved bitter and protracted fighting. Raleigh Trevelyan, who was at Anzio with the Rifle Brigade, has published a memorable account of his experiences under the title of *The Fortress* (1956).

Tune: 'Lachlan Tigers' (otherwise known as 'The Knickerbocker Line')

> When the MGs stop their chatter and the cannons stop their roar,
> And you're back in dear old Blighty in your favourite pub once more;
> When the small talk is all over and the war tales start to flow,
> You can stop the lot by telling of the fight at Anzio.

Let them bum about the desert, let them talk about Dunkirk,
Let them brag about the jungles where the Japanese did lurk.
Let them boast about their campaign and their medals till they glow,
You can put the lot to silence when you mention Anzio.

You can tell of Anzio Archie and the factory where the Huns
Used to ask us out to breakfast as they rubbed against our guns.
You can talk of night patrolling they knew nothing of at home,
And tell them that you learned it on the beachhead south of Rome.

You can tell them how the Heinkels tried to break us with attacks,
Using tanks and bombs and cannons, and how we flung them back.
You can tell them how we took it and dished it out as well,
How we thought it was a picnic and *tedeschi* thought it hell.

And when the tale is finished and going time is near,
Just fill your pipes again, lads, and finish up your beer.
Then order up another pint and drink before you go
To the boys that fought beside you on the beach at Anzio.

ᴄᴇ · *D-DAY DODGERS* · ᴅᴏ

This was more or less universally known to British, American and Canadian soldiers who served in Italy in 1944 and 1945. It was written in November 1944 by Lance-Sergeant Harry Pynn of the Tank Rescue Section, 19 Army Fire Brigade, who was with the 79th Division which had at that time been battling for three months against the German Gothic Line, a series of fortified positions running across Italy south of Bologna.

The song sets out to respond to the allegation that the troops in Italy were enjoying an easy option. This view was popularly believed to have originated with Lady Astor (1879–1964), Conservative MP for Plymouth from 1919 until 1945, who is said to have expressed exasperation in the House of Commons at the Eighth Army's delay in breaking through the Gothic Line, and drawn an unfavourable comparison with the efforts of the D-Day forces in France. An alternative story is that, as a member of a parliamentary delegation visiting Italy in October 1944 she voiced similar sentiments, adding that the troops were drunken, dissolute and oversexed. Documentation of such remarks is wanting, and Lady Astor herself strenuously denied making them. She was nevertheless well known for her *hauteur*, and the popular view stuck. Oddly enough, she does not feature in Pynn's original text, but is almost invariably mentioned in other versions. Three verses on her illustrate the many variations which the text underwent:

> Now Lady Astor, get a load of this:
> Don't stand on a platform and talk a load of piss.
> You're the nation's sweetheart, the nation's pride,
> But your mouth's too bleeding wide,
> For we are the D-Day dodgers in sunny Italy.

> Oh Lady Astor, listen please to us,
> Don't get on a platform and make a bloody fuss.
> We know you were the services' sweetheart and pride;
> You opened your mouth a bit too wide.
> We were the D-Day dodgers, the boys who D-Day dodge.

> You've heard of Lady Astor, our pin-up girl out here,
> She is the dear old lady who tries to stop our beer;
> And when we get our Astor band
> We'll be the proudest in the land,
> We are the D-Day dodgers, way out in Italy.

The tune chosen undoubtedly helped the song to catch on, and become popular. It was 'Lili Marlene'. The words for this were written in 1915 by Hans Leip, while serving on the Russian front in the German Army, but not published until a volume of his poems, *Die Hafenorgel* [*The Harbour Organ*], came out in 1937. A year later it was set to music by Norbert Schultze, and recorded in Germany by Lale Andersen just before the outbreak of war. When this was broadcast to the Afrika Korps in 1941 it became a huge success, not only with the troops for whom it was intended, but with British soldiers of the Eighth Army who also listened in. The Germans quickly realised the song's potential, as they thought, for sapping the Tommies' will to win, and played the song across no man's land every night through loudspeakers. The British quickly evolved their own versions of the words:

> There was a song that the Eighth Army used to hear
> In the lonely desert, lovely, sweet and clear.
> Over the ether came the strain,
> The soft refrain each night again,
> With you, Lili Marlene, with you, Lili Marlene.

After the defeat of Rommel a further verse was added:

> Afrika Korps has vanished from the earth,
> Smashed soon the swine that gave it birth.
> No more you'll hear that lilting strain,
> That soft refrain each night again,
> With you, Lili Marlene, with you, Lili Marlene.

An official English version was written by Tommy Connor and published in 1944, then recorded by Anne Shelton in England and Marlene Dietrich in the United

Lance-sergeant Harry Pynn, Tank Rescue Section, 19th Army Fire Brigade, 1944. Pynn wrote the song on page 180

States. Meanwhile, the 'Lili Marlene' tune was being used for other soldiers' songs, too, and 'D-Day Dodgers' was spreading through the army.

Of the places in Italy mentioned, Salerno and Anzio were the sites of landings in September 1943 and January 1944 respectively. Sangro, a river in southern Italy, was reached by the Eighth Army in November 1943, but crossed only after heavy fighting. Ortona and Pescara are towns on the Adriatic coast. Cassino was a battleground from January to May in 1944.

Tune: 'Lili Marlene'

> We are D-Day dodgers, out in Italy,
> Always drinking vino, always on the spree;
> Eighth Army skivers with 5th Yanks,
> We stroll in Rome far from the tanks,
> For we are only D-Day dodgers, out in Italy.
>
> Some landed at Salerno, a holiday with pay,
> And Jerry came to meet us to cheer us on our way.
> We all sat round with cakes and tea,
> And after that the beer was free,
> For we are only D-Day dodgers, out in Italy.
>
> The muddy river Sangro was looking quite forlorn;
> We didn't force a crossing there, we slept from dusk till dawn.
> We then loped about to kill the time,
> Then took a stroll through the Gothic Line,
> For we are only D-Day dodgers, out in Italy.
>
> Ortona and Pescara were taken in our stride,
> We didn't go to fight there, we just went for the ride.
> Then to Cassino we did go,
> And others went to Anzio,
> For we are only D-Day dodgers, out in Italy.
>
> Once we heard a rumour we were going home,
> Back to dear old Blighty, never more to roam,
> But they said in France you will have to fight;
> We said, 'Damn that, we'll just sit tight,
> For we are only D-Day dodgers, out in Italy.'
>
> We heard the boys in France were going home on leave,
> After five months' service there it's time they were relieved,
> But we'll soldier on for months and years;
> Our wives at home shed no more tears,
> For we are only D-Day dodgers, out in Italy.

Troops landing at Salerno docks, September 1943

If you wander through the mountains or across the dusty plains,
You'll find a lot of crosses, some that bear no names.
These were our comrades slumbering on,
And we who are left will sing this song,
We are the D-Day dodgers, out in Italy.

Now Winston Churchill, give us leave at home,
Now we have captured Naples, Florence, Rome.
We'll come back and beat the master race,
And Grigg has got some shipping space,
Oh please let us see home, oh please let us see home.

◦ *SOUTH OF MEIKTILA* ·

The 9th Battalion of the Border Regiment, which went to Burma in July 1943, was involved in particularly heavy fighting during the campaign of 1945 to capture Mandalay and Rangoon from the Japanese. The song mentions Meiktila (taken in March) and Pyawbe, thirty miles south (taken in April), but deals more with engagements in various villages in between. 'Long John', so called because he was tall and thin, was Major (later Lieutenant-Colonel) John Petty, MBE, MC. Major R. B. Patch was awarded the MC for his part in one of the actions. 'Tommo' refers to Major J. A. Thompson, a wartime officer and later Cumbrian farmer and teacher. The song was written by Sergeant Tommy Wren, and sung for the first time at a battalion concert party at Waw, near the Sittang River, in September 1945.

The popular song 'South of the Border' served as a model for several soldiers' compositions, including 'South of Colombo' and 'South of the Sangro'.

Tune: 'South of the Border'

> South of Meiktila, down Pyawbe way,
> That's where the Japs thought that they had come to stay.
> The Borders surprised them one sunny day,
> South of Meiktila, down Pyawbe way.
>
> Then in went 'B' Company, led by Long John,
> And Major Patch, MC, took 'A' Company along.
> 'C' Company behind them with Tommo in charge;
> 'D' were right forward, near the barrage.
>
> Then the Japs started shouting and screaming
> When the mortar platoon got weaving,
> But the boys didn't need any screening,
> Oh for the Japs were on the run.
>
> South of Meiktila, down Pyawbe way,
> That's where the CO said, 'You all salute to the front today.'
> Fifty Div. passed through us on to Toungoo;
> Two-sixty flanked us by taking Rangoon.

ᑕᕽᕋ · *THE DYING SOLDIER* · ᕋᕽᕐ

Kohima is on the Indo-Burmese border. A probably earlier version of this Second World War song places the action in the Middle instead of the Far East. The subject is merely 'a young British soldier', and Kohima, Japanese and Burma and replaced respectively by Benghazi, Eyetie and Africa. 'Out in the jungle' becomes 'deep in the desert'.

Tune: 'Red River Valley' or 'Eton Boating Song'

A.
'Twas out at that place called Kohima
Where most of the fighting was done;
'Twas there that a lad from the Borders
Fell to a Japanese gun.

Now as he lay there in the jungle,
And the blood from his wounds did flow red,
He gathered his comrades around him,
And these were the words that he said.

'Oh bury me out in the jungle
Under the old Burma sun;
Bury me out in the jungle,
My duty to England is done.'

So they buried him out in the jungle
By the light of the far setting sun;
They buried him out in the jungle,
His job for his country was done.

Now when you get back to old England,
And the war is all over and won,
Just remember that poor British Tommy,
Under the old Burma sun.

Now if she had only been faithful
He might have been raising a son,
But instead he's just pushing up teak trees
Under the old Burma sun.

A further version (B) reworks the song in terms of a paratrooper.

B.
Oh come sit by my side if you love me,
Do not hasten to bid me adieu,
But remember the poor paratrooper
And the job he is trying to do.

When the red light comes on we are ready
For the sergeant to shout: 'Number One'.
Though we sit in the plane all together,
We all tumble out one by one.

When we're coming in for a landing,
Just remember the sergeant's advice:
Keep your feet and your knees close together,
And you'll reach Mother Earth very nice.

When we land in a certain country,
There's a job we will do very well.
We will fire old Goering and Adolf,
And all of those blighters as well.

So stand by your glass and be ready,
And remember the men of the sky.
Here's a toast to the men dead already,
And a toast for the next man to die.

Operation Market Garden:
paratroops leaving (opposite) and en route for Arnhem, September 1944

⚬ · DISCHARGE SONG · ⚭

This powerful expression of longing for release from military servitude was widely sung by Australian soldiers in the Second World War and afterwards.

Tune: 'Home on the Range'

> Oh give me a home where no army can roam,
> Where no brasshats or provosts can stay,
> Where there's no dress parades or no more air raids,
> And no adjutants to forfeit your pay.
>
> Oh give me a land which I know I can stand,
> Where I won't be annoyed by those stripes.
> No more waiting in queues while they fill me with stews,
> And rice puddings that give me the gripes.
>
> Now I've found that home where no army can roam,
> Bully beef is a thing of the past.
> Though the atmosphere's hot in this new home I've got,
> I'm out of the army at last.

⚬ · AFRICA STAR · ⚭

Campaign medals do not always command the respect of the troops, as this bitter song of the Second World War shows. It was sung by both soldiers and airmen. Lady Astor (verse three) was distinctly unpopular with servicemen (see also 'D-Day Dodgers', page 180). Shepheard's Bazaar (verse four) is in Cairo.

Tune: 'Home on the Range'

> Oh give me a bar to my Africa Star
> And a clasp to pin on my breast,
> Then I'll stay here in base with a smile on my face,
> Content on my laurels to rest.

(Chorus)
Star, beautiful star,
I'd rather have beer by far.
If you've an akker or two
I'll have Stella with you
While I tell how I won my Star.

Distribution was wide, it spread like a tide,
Like the leaves that come down in the fall,
For as you can see they gave one to me
And to NAFFI and ENSA and all.

Lady Astor herself has one on the shelf
To wear when she puts on her togs.
If you look down the list the only ones they missed
Were the Jerries, the Eyeties, the dogs.

Oh give me a bar in my homeland afar
Where I can show off my Africa Star,
And then I'll confess before they all guess
That I bought it in Shepheard's Bazaar.

Piper MacDonald of the Seaforth Highlanders leading a section in the North African desert, September 1942

Bill ('Pop') Hingston of the Devonshire Regiment at Port Said, 1949. Hingston (see page 140) as a noted singer

· I DON'T WANT MY · NAME ON A CENOTAPH

The soldier's deep longing to escape from all things military and to return to civilian life is again expressed in this song of the Second World War.

Tune: 'The Eton Boating Song'

Oh I don't want my name on a cenotaph
In letters of shining gold,
For that won't be much use to me
When I'm lying stiff and cold.
Let the others all laugh at me
And say that I was afraid.
It is I who will have the last laugh,
I'll be first on the last parade.

I'll stay up all the night before,
For I know that I sha'n't sleep.
I'll polish my brasses, shine my boots,
Fold up my bed nice and neat;
And early the next morning
I'll be ready with a nice clean shave:
There'll be plenty of competition,
But I'll be first on the last parade.

And when this war is over
And we've all got a nice big ale,
And when it comes round to my turn
To pay for drinks and tell the tale,
I'll tell them the old story,
How through mud and blood I did wade;
But the sergeant will shout: 'You liar.
You were first on the last parade.'

ᴄᴇ · *THE '39–'45 STAR* · ᴅᴏ

The veteran soldier is quite capable of feeling contempt for medals, which are trivial when compared with the sweat and blood he has expended and the time he has served.

Tune: 'Alice Blue Gown'

> It's the thirty-nine–forty-five star,
> It's the best little ribbon so far.
> I've got one on my chest
> And one on my vest,
> And one on my pyjamas when I go to rest.
> It's the thirty-nine–forty-five star,
> It's the best little ribbon so far;
> But I doubt if I'll wear it,
> There's too many to share it,
> The thirty-nine–forty-five star.

(e) After 1945

ROLL ON THE BOAT

When you're standing on the square,
And you hear the sergeant swear;
When he shouts, 'Get in line there,'
Roll on the boat.

He shouts out, 'What's the matter, Smith?
I'll move you in half a jiff.
Your shoulders are skew-wiff.'
Roll on the boat.

When the sergeant shouts out, 'Shun.
It's a rifle you've got, not a gun.
Take that man's name – the second one.'
Roll on the boat.

To the company commander you wend your way.
He says, 'Well, what have you got to say?
That's enough. Send him away.'
Roll on the boat.

When you get your ticket, all is well.
You're sailing home with news to tell.
You can tell the sergeant he can go to hell.
At last, the boat.

In civvy street you're classed a failure.
When you owe a lot to butcher and tailor
You hop it quick before they can nail yer.
Roll on death, life's a failure.

· SPUD SPEDDING'S ·
BROKEN BOYS

This somewhat wry valediction was sung by members of the Border Regiment while on a tour of duty in Burma from 1945 to 1946. Lieutenant-Colonel Spedding commanded the regiment's ninth battalion from the Battle of Imphal in March 1944, and remained in charge after its amalgamation with the fourth in 1945. A former member of the regiment, Major Patch (who is mentioned in the song on page 182) remembered the title as 'Spud Spedding's Border Boys', but neither he nor anyone else I have been able to consult could recall the tune. 'Spud' is a generic nickname for anyone called Spedding. For Minden dandies, see page 194.

I was walking down the street the other day,
When I chanced to hear a certain lady say:
'Why isn't he in khaki or a suit of navy blue,
Fighting for his country like other fellows do?'

I turned around, and this is what I said:
'Now, lady, look. I've only got one leg.
On two legs I'd be firmer, but the other one's out in Burma.
I'm one of Spud Spedding's broken boys.'

Now it appeared on Orders that I should join the Borders,
To be one of Spud Spedding's broken boys.
So seeing I was willing they packed me off to Bilin,
To be one of Spud Spedding's broken boys.

Now I hadn't been there long when they sent me to Taungzun,
'Cause I'm one, *etc.*
I thought I was going home but they ordered us to Prome,
We're some of, *etc.*

But we hadn't finished yet, you know, for they sent us to Thayetmyo,
'Cause we are, *etc.*
Poor lad, his name was Andy, he became a Minden Dandy,
He's one, *etc.*

We saw the rations through at Milestone twenty-two,
We're some, *etc.*
And if I'd been a farmer I might have gone to Kama,
Like some of, *etc.*

And I think they got it wrong: 'No guns at Shwemaungzaung.'
I'm one of, *etc.*
Yes, we caught them single-handed, but now the mob's disbanded,
And where are, *etc.*?

Now if I'd tried rather harder I'd have made the UK cadre,
And stayed with, *etc.*
But I sadly packed my bedding and I left the ranks of Spedding,
We're no longer, *etc.*

And I never even thought that we'd get to 'Churchill Court',
But then we're, *etc.*
They caught a *dhobi wallah* throwing bombs in Maniktolla
At some of, *etc.*
And they say a rubber dingy is no use on Chowringhee,
To some of, *etc.*

For the army we were hired, but now we're time expired,
So here's to Spud Spedding's broken boys.

Members of the 1st Border Regiment embarking for home on the Empire Ken *at Port Said, December 1954*

ᯓ · *THE MINDEN* · ᯓ
DANDIES

Members of the Border Regiment sang these words in Burma in 1946, though the first two verses clearly refer to the Royal Welch Fusiliers. Minden (1759) was one of the battle honours of the RWF, and the regiment was known as 'The Flash' (and hence, perhaps, the dandies) from the distinctive bunch of black ribbon worn at the back collar of the tunic as a relic of the queue or pigtail.

Tune: medley, including 'Follow the Band'

> We are the Minden dandies, straight from the west,
> Some of the latest and some of the best.
> We join in royally wherever we go,
> But where we come from nobody knows.
>
> They call us the pride of the ladies, the ladies,
> They take all our wages, our wages, our wages.
> We are respected wherever we roam,
> We are the Minden dandies.
>
> Down by the Irra-Irrawaddy you can hear the Burmese sing,
> Takes my heart right back
> To a little bamboo *basha* by the Waddy's shore,
> A place to call our own.
> Oh I love to sit and listen, to hear the Burmese singing
> Home, sweet home.

ᯓ · *MOVING ON* · ᯓ

Several classic themes combine in this song of the Korean War (1950–52). The lonely soldier feels that he is fighting someone else's war. In addition his wife at home has left him, and a woman in Korea has given him venereal disease. Synghman Rhee was the corrupt dictator brought back in the baggage train of the allies, and restored to power in South Korea.

See an old leave train coming down the track,
An Aussie on the front and a Yankee on the back.
(*Chorus*)
I'm moving on; I'll soon be gone.
I'd like to stay but the MPs say:
'Keep moving on.'

I had a girl down in Seoul;
She kept treating me like a fool.

If I heard that bastard Synghman Rhee
Say one word of thanks to me.

I got a letter from my home
Said my old girl's got another man.
She's moving on, etc.

I had a girl and she was willing,
Now I'm taking penicillin.

Sexy, sexy, stick or bust.
If the Yanks don't get you the women must.

Roll call of survivors of the 1st Battalion, Gloucestershire Regiment, after the battle of Solma Ri, Korea, 1951

Drawing by Harry Hall published in the Toronto Telegram *after the battle of the Imjin River, Korea, 1951*

· GHOST ARMY OF · KOREA

Service during the Korean War was on the whole decidedly unpopular. It is said that the song was officially banned in British units, but that handwritten copies were defiantly fly-posted in NAAFI canteens, including that of the Gloucestershire Regiment. The text seems to be partly based on 'We've Done Our Hitch in Hell', a song of the Spanish-American War of 1898 which concludes:

When the final taps are sounded and we lay aside life's cares;
When we do the last parade, boys, upon the golden stairs;
When the angels bid us welcome and the harps begin to play;
'Tis then we'll hear the bugle calling to that great and happy day.
Then St Peter'll tell the angels how we charged and how we fell:
'Give a front seat to the Third Wyoming for they've done their hitch in hell.'

Tune: based on 'Botany Bay'

Just below the Manchurian border, Korea's the name of the spot.
We're due to be spending our time here in the land that God forgot.

Down with the snakes and the lizards, down where the swaddy is blue,
Right in the middle of nowhere, and thousands of miles from you.

We sweat, we freeze and we shiver; it's more than a man can bear.
We're not a bunch of convicts, we are only doing our share.

Living with photos and memories, dreaming sometimes of our gals,
Hoping that while we have been away they have not married our pals.

Few people know what we're doing and few people give a damn;
Although we are almost forgotten we belong to the khaki clan.

We are soldiers of the army, earning our measly pay;
Guarding over millionaires for four lousy shillings a day.

The good times we've had in the army and the good times we have missed;
Here's hoping the army don't get you, so for Christ's sake don't go and enlist.

And when we arrive in heaven St Peter will surely tell
They've just come back from Korea, dear God, they've been serving their time
in hell.

⤳ · SEVEN NIGHTS · ⤳
DRUNK

This was first printed in the eighteenth century as 'Our Goodman', and remained in oral circulation to the present day. A truncated version sung by the Dubliners reached the Top Twenty in the 1960s. Soldiers sang it at least until the 1950s; Gordon Hall's version is given here. The words in italics are repeated in almost every verse.

Oh as I came home one Monday *night, as drunk as drunk could be,*
Well, I saw a horse outside the door *where my old* horse *should be.*
I called the wife and said to her, 'Will you kindly tell to me
Who owns that horse outside the door *where my old* horse *should be?'*
'Ah, you're drunk, you're drunk, you silly old fool. Surely you can see
That's a lovely milking cow *my mother gave to me.'*
'Well, it's many a day I've travelled, a hundred miles or more,
But a milking cow with a saddle on *I never saw before.'*

Tuesday . . . a coat behind the door
Woollen blanket . . . buttons in a blanket

Wednesday . . . pipe beside the bed
Lovely tin whistle . . . tobacco in a tin whistle

Thursday . . . two boots beside the bed
Two lovely geranium pots . . . laces in geranium pots

Friday . . . head upon the bed
Baby boy . . . a baby boy with his whiskers on

Saturday . . . stain upon the counterpane
Drop of the baby's milk . . . baby's milk that smelt like come

Sunday . . . an old tool upon the bed
Lovely carrot . . . a carrot with a pair of balls

 · THE REME SONG ·

Between the late 1950s and at least the mid-1970s this song circulated among members of BAOR. Among several variations was 'LAD [Light Aid Detachment] boys' for 'dreamy REME'. The rank of craftsman (verse four) is the REME equivalent of private.

Tune: 'Lili Marlene'

Early in the morning, workshop on parade,
Here comes the sergeant-major to the 'Donkey Serenade'.
Some silly bastard shouts 'Right dress';
You should have seen the fucking mess.
We are the dreamy REME, we are a bloody shower.

Down in the NAAFI beer-bar, twenty pints an hour,
We are the dreamy REME, we are a bloody shower.
We pick them up and we drink them down,
Pissed as a newt on half-a-crown,
We are the dreamy REME, we are a bloody shower.

Cruising down the autobahn at fifty miles an hour,
We are the dreamy REME, we are a bloody shower.
We can't change up and we can't change down –
The gearbox is in but it's upside down,
We are the dreamy REME in sunny Germany.

We pulled it and we pushed it, we stripped the bastard down,
There were bits and pieces scattered all around.
Up walked a craftsman with a petrol can;
We stood and cried what we had done.
We are the dreamy REME, we are a bloody shower.

· THE SOLDIER ·

In 1971 in Belfast a soldier called Sergeant Willis cleared a room of civilians because of a bomb. As he went to close the door afterwards, the charge exploded, and he was killed. A professional songwriter, Harvey Andrews, was so struck by the incident that he wrote the song to make the point that soldiers, too, are human. (The incident of the soldier's embracing the bomb was poetic licence.)

Broadcasts of Andrews' record were banned for some time by the BBC lest feelings be exacerbated in the nationalist community of Northern Ireland. The Ministry of Defence advised (and still advises) soldiers not to sing the song in pubs where it might cause trouble. Some have interpreted this as a ban. Nevertheless, they sing it 'all the time', according to one source, on military transport and in messes and canteens. It has been said that some units require newcomers to learn to sing or recite the song before they become fully accepted.

Andrews' authorship is not widely known, and many different stories about the song's origin circulate: the writer served with 2 Para or the SAS; it was the work of an ordinary soldier who wished to remain anonymous; it was written by a prisoner in the course of his rehabilitation. The text has appeared in the *Soldier*, the *Methodist* magazine, and the *Manchester Evening News* (where in 1988 it won a poetry competition for a youth who sent it in over his own name).

This divorce of a song from its maker and its establishment as common property, together with the emergence of different versions, are classic signs of the process through which folk songs evolve. On a train in 1982 Lyn Macdonald met a young soldier who wrote down the text of the song for her. She next saw him on the television three months later as he marched through the streets of Port Stanley.

The tune is by Harvey Andrews.

In a station in the city a British soldier stood,
Talking to the people there if the people would.
Some just stared in hatred and others turned in pain,
And the lonely British soldier wished he was back home again.

'Come join the British Army,' said the posters in his town.
'See the world and have your fun, come serve before the crown.'
The jobs were hard to come by and he could not face the dole,
So he took his country's shilling and enlisted on the roll.

But there was no fear of fighting, the empire long was lost.
Just ten years in the army getting paid for being bossed,
Then leave, a man experienced, a man who's made the grade:
A medal and a pension, some memories and a trade.

Then came the call to Ireland as the call had come before,
Another bloody chapter in an endless civil war.
The priests they stood on both sides, the priests they stood behind:
Another fight in Jesus' name, the blind against the blind.

The soldier stood between them, between the whistling stones,
And then the broken bottles that led to broken bones,
The petrol bombs that burned his hands, the nails that pierced his skin,
And wished that he had stayed at home surrounded by his kin.

The station filled with people, the soldier soon was bored,
But better in the station than where the people warred.
The room filled up with mothers, with daughters and with sons,
Who stared with itchy fingers at the soldier and his guns.

A yell of fear, a screech of brakes, a shattering of glass:
The window of the station broke to let the package pass.
A scream came from the mothers as they ran towards the door,
Dragging children crying from the bomb upon the floor.

The soldier stood and could not move, his gun he could not use;
He knew the bomb had seconds and not minutes on the fuse.
He could not run to pick it up and throw it in the street:
There were far too many people there, too many running feet.

'Take cover,' yelled the soldier, 'take cover for your lives,'
And the Irishmen threw down their young and stood before their wives.
They turned towards the soldier, their eyes alive with fear:
'For God's sake, save our children or they'll end their short lives here.'

The soldier moved towards the bomb, his stomach like a stone.
Why was this his battle? God, why was he alone?
He lay down on the package and he murmured one farewell
To those at home in England, to those he loved so well.

He saw the sights of summer, felt the wind upon his brow.
The young girls in the city parks, how precious were they now.
The soaring of the swallow, the beauty of the swan,
The music of the turning earth, so soon it would be gone.

A muffled, soft explosion, and the floor began to quake;
The soldier blown across the room, his blood a crimson lake.
They never heard him cry or shout, they never heard him moan,
And they turned their children's faces from the blood and from the bone.

The crowd outside soon gathered and the ambulances came
To carry off the body of a pawn lost to the game,
And the crowd they clapped and jeered, and they sang their rebel song:
One soldier less to interfere where he did not belong.

But will the children growing up learn at their mother's knee
The story of the soldier who bought their liberty?
Who used his youthful body as the means towards the end,
Who gave his life to those who called him 'murderer', not 'friend'?

Ꮼ · NOW THAT YOU'RE · ᎗᎗
AN ARMY WIFE

For centuries army wives have shared the hardships of their menfolk in barracks, on campaign, and even in battle. That danger and even death can still threaten them was demonstrated by the murder of a soldier's wife by the IRA in Germany in 1989.

Two other wives wrote this song not about peril but about parting, loneliness, and the common problems of being married to soldiers. Canterbury is the home town of the Queen's Regiment, to which the women's husbands belong. The men returned from a four-month tour of duty in West Belfast on 12 September 1988. 'R and R' means 'rest and recuperation'; 'LOA' means 'local overseas allowance' (paid in Germany, but not in Northern Ireland).

Tune: 'Cottonfields'

Now that you're an army wife you're going to have to change your life,
Lonely days and all those lonely nights.
Endless nights without the men – when's he coming home again?
Lonely days and all those lonely nights.

And as you wave him out the door
He's off on another Ireland tour.
All those letters he promises to send,
And R and R was short and sweet.
As the tears roll down your cheeks
You wonder when, oh when, will all this end.

Endless cleaning of the quarter, Windolene and soapy water,
Washing up and hoovering the floor,
And tempers start to fray as the kids get in the way.
'Daddy, please don't go away no more.'

And as you wave him out the door
He's off on another Ireland tour.
All those letters he promises to send.
Darling, please will you come home?
'Cause I don't want to be alone.
I wonder when, oh when, will this all end.

When another posting's due the army knows what's best for you.
You're left, you're left wondering where it's gonna be;
And as the rumours start to spread
As you're lying in your bed
You're thinking: 'Canterbury's the place for me.'

And as you wave him out the door
He's off on another Ireland tour.
All those letters he promises to send.
We're gonna lose our LOA
'Cause we're posted to UK,
And now we're wondering where it's gonna end.

If you think an army wife has a free and easy life,
Think again. It couldn't be more wrong,
For although we have each other, we stick by one another,
And our message is written in this song.

And as you greet him at the door
He's back from another Ireland tour.
All those letters he promised that he'd send.
Though it's been so hard to smile,
Now you're smiling all the while,
'Cause you're together, together to the end.

Twelfth of September this tour is at an end.

· *NOTE ON TUNES* ·

Ideally, one would have liked to print the tunes of all the songs. To have done so would have increased the price of the book to a prohibitively high level. Wherever possible the titles of tunes used are indicated. When an original tune or variant is used by the singer I have shown in the Notes on Sources where either a printed or recorded version of the music can be found.

This still leaves some tunes difficult to trace, especially where material is previously unpublished. A cassette with a selection of songs from the book, sung by their original singers, has been prepared by John Howson of Veteran Tapes, 44 Old Street, Haughley, Stowmarket, Suffolk IP14 2NX (catalogue number VT121). Any reader who is still unable to find the tune of one of these songs and is particularly anxious to do so is invited to write to me, care of the publisher.

· ABBREVIATIONS ·

Blackmore MS
Manuscript Book of Songs, Poems and Jokes, compiled in India in 1937 by William Blackmore of the 1st Devonshire Regiment, and now in the possession of Mrs Baker of Topsham, Devon. A photocopy in the Folklore Centre, Topsham, Devon, was kindly communicated by the Director, Sam Richards.

Brophy and Partridge
John Brophy and Eric Partridge, *The Long Trail: Soldiers' Songs and Slang, 1914–1918* (4th ed. André Deutsch, 1965; orig. published in 1930 as *Songs and Slang of the British Soldier*).

Bundook
Ewan MacColl, *Bundook Ballads*, 12″ LP record, Topic 12T130 (1958).

Coppard
George Coppard, *With a Machine Gun to Cambrai* (HMSO, 1969).

Coppard Tape
Tape recorded at George Coppard's home in Hastings in 1983 in connection with my adaptation for BBC Radio of his book.

Cox
Gordon Cox, 'Songs and Ballads of the Wet Canteen: Recollections of a British Soldier [John Gregson] in India', *Lore and Language*, 3, no. 7 (1982), 53–67.

Cray
Ed Cray (ed.), *Bawdy Ballads* (Anthony Blond, 1970).

Dallas
Karl Dallas (ed.), *The Cruel Wars. 100 Soldiers' Songs from Agincourt to Ulster* (Wolfe, 1972).

Dolph
Edward Arthur Dolph (ed.), *Sound Off! Soldier Songs from the Revolution to World War II* (New York, Farrar and Rinehart, 1942).

Gregson Tape
Songs sung by John Gregson of Burnley, Lancs.; recorded by Gordon Cox, 1977, and kindly communicated by him.

Giraud
S. Louis Giraud (ed.), *Songs that Won the War* (Lane Publications, 1930).

Hall Tapes
Five cassettes of songs sung by Gordon Hall of Sussex and other members of his family; recorded, 1989, by Gordon Hall, and kindly communicated by him.

Henderson
Hamish Henderson, *Ballads of World War II* (Glasgow, Lili Marlene Club, n.d.).

Hewins
Angela Hewins (ed.), *The Dillen: Memories of a Man of Stratford-upon-Avon* (Elm Tree Books, 1981).

Hopkins
Anthony Hopkins (ed.), *Songs from the Front and Rear: Canadian Servicemen's Songs from the Second World War* (Edmonton, Canada, Hurtig, 1979).

Huggett
Frank E. Huggett, *Goodnight Sweetheart: Songs and Memories of the Second World War* (W. H. Allen, 1979).

Lomax

John A. and Alan Lomax (eds), *American Ballads and Folk Songs* (New York, 1949; orig. 1934).

Macdonald (1984)

Lyn Macdonald, *Somme* (Macmillan, 1984).

Macdonald (1989)

Lyn Macdonald, *1914* (Penguin, 1989).

Matthews Tape

Cassette of songs learnt during army service in the Second World War by S. A. ('Nibs') Matthews of London, 1987, and kindly communicated by him.

Mays

Spike Mays, *Fall out the Officers* (Eyre and Spottiswoode, 1969).

Mays (1986)

Spike Mays, *Return to Anglia* (1986).

Nettleingham

F. T. Nettleingham (ed.), *Tommy's Tunes: a Comprehensive Collection of Soldiers' Songs, Marching Melodies, Rude Rhymes and Popular Parodies, Composed, Collected and Arranged on Active Service with the B.E.F.* (Erskine Macdonald, 1917).

Nettleingham

F. T. Nettleingham (ed.), *More Tommy's Tunes: an Additional Collection*, etc. (Erskine Macdonald, 1918).

Page (1973)

Martin Page (ed.), *Kiss Me Goodnight Sergeant-Major: The Songs and Ballads of World War II* (Hart-Davis, MacGibbon, 1973)

Page (1976)

Martin Page (ed.), *For Gawd's Sake Don't Take Me: Songs, Ballads, Verses, Monologues, etc. of the Call-Up Years, 1939–1963* (Hart-Davis, MacGibbon, 1976).

Palmer

Roy Palmer (ed.), *The Rambling Soldier* (Penguin, 1977; Sutton, 1985).

Seeger and MacColl

Peggy Seeger and Ewan MacColl (eds), *The Singing Island: A Collection of English and Scots Folksongs* (Mills Music, 1960).

Stoke Tapes

Tapes of the reminiscences and songs of Stoke-on-Trent men who were held as prisoners-of-war by the Germans and/or Italians during the Second World War: Bill Arnitt, Jock Attrill, Reg Baker, Frank Bayley, Bob Burt, Jack Ford, John Hamilton, Eric Wilson and Arthur Winkle. The recordings were made by members of the Victoria Theatre, Stoke, in connection with *Hands Up – For You the War is Ended*, a musical documentary staged in 1971. I am most grateful to the director, Peter Cheeseman, for communicating these tapes.

Tawney

Cyril Tawney, *Grey Funnel Lines: Traditional Song and Verse of the Royal Navy, 1900–1970* (Routledge, 1987).

Up in Arms

The Yetties, *Up in Arms*, 12″ LP record, Argo ZDA 100 (1974).

Ward-Jackson

C. H. Ward-Jackson and Leighton Lucas (eds), *Airman's Song Book: Being an Anthology of Squadron, Concert Party, Training and Camp Songs and Song-Parodies, written by and for Officers, Airmen and Airwomen mainly of the Royal Air Force, its Auxiliaries and its Predecessors the Royal Flying Corps and the Royal Naval Air Service* (William Blackwood, 1967).

Williamson

Henry Williamson, *The Patriot's Progress* (Bles, 1930).

Wilson
L. M. B. Wilson (ed.), *Regimental Music of the Queen's Regiment* (privately printed, 1980).
Winstock
Lewis Winstock, *Songs and Music of the Redcoats: A History of the War Music of the British Army, 1642–1902* (Leo Cooper, 1970).
de Witt
Hugh de Witt (ed.), *Bawdy Barrack-room Ballads* (1970).

· NOTES ON ·
INTRODUCTION

For full details of references given in abbreviated form, see page 206.

1. Quoted in *Grove's Musical Dictionary* (Oxford University Press, 5th ed.), article, 'Military Calls', p. 774.
2. From Harold Wirdnam of Newent, Glos., 1989.
3. From my father, who served in the Leicestershire Regiment in the 1920s.
4. *Newsletter*, Regimental Association, Queen's Royal Surrey Regiment, no. 19 (May 1976), 6. Cf. *Trumpet and Bugle Calls for the Army* (War Department, 1966), no. 106.
5. As note 3. Cf. *Trumpet and Bugle Calls*, no. 119.
6. As note 4, no. 18 (November 1975). Cf. Nettleingham (1917), no. 66, and *Trumpet and Bugle Calls*, no. 117.
7. As note 6. Cf. *Trumpet and Bugle Calls*, no. 89.
8. Mays (1969), p. 48.
9. Gregson Tape. Cf. article cited in note 1, p. 778, and *Trumpet and Bugle Calls*, no. 59.
10. Gregson Tape.
11. Rudyard Kipling, *Barrack Room Ballads* (1892). The poem was set to music by A. Campbell Geddes (*The British Students' Song Book* [n.d.], p. 94).
12. Patrick MacGill, *Soldier Songs* (Herbert Jenkins, 1917), pp. 90–1.
13. Edmund Blunden, *Undertones of War* (Cobden-Sanderson, 1928), pp. 151 and 247.
14. Robert Graves, *Goodbye to All That* (Penguin, 1960), p. 125.
15. Coppard, pp. 50–1.
16. Hall Tapes.
17. Macdonald (1984), p. 200.
18. *Ibid.*, pp. 201–2.
19. As note 16.
20. Brophy and Partridge, p. 6.
21. Frank Richards, *Old Soldiers Never Die* (Faber, 1954), p. 85.
22. Blunden, *Undertones*, p. 136.
23. Personal communication, 10 March 1987.
24. Stoke Tapes.
25. Blunden, *Undertones*, p. 52. For a full text of the song, see Bon Pegg, *Folk* (Wildwood House, 1976), pp. 84–5.
26. J. H. Bassett, contribution to the book, *The Distant Drum: Reflections on the Spanish Civil War*, ed. Philip Toynbee (Sidgwick and Jackson, 1976), p. 135.

27. Nettleingham (1917), p. 6.
28. Quoted in Macdonald (1989), pp. 396–7.
29. Coppard Tape.
30. Nettleingham (1917), p. 7.
31. Personal communication, 26 November 1986.
32. Personal communication, 27 September 1976.
33. Quoted in Cox, p. 58.
34. Author's Tape, 1989.
35. Hall Tapes. For a version of 'King Farouk', see Page (1973), p. 84.
36. Brophy and Partridge, pp. 27, 46 and 55.
37. Nettleingham (1917), p. 10.
38. Ivor Gurney, *War Letters*, edited by R. K. R. Thornton (Hogarth Press, 1984), p. 38.
39. John Brophy and Eric Partridge, *Songs and Slang of the British Soldier* (1930), p. 15.
40. J. B. Priestley, *Margin Released* (Heinemann, 1962), p. 111. 'We don't want to lose you' can be heard in full on the record, *Keep the Home Fires Burning* (Saydisc SDL358, 1986). This song was parodied as 'I'm sick of this blooming war' (Nettleingham (1917), no. 20).
41. MacGill, *Soldier Songs*, pp. 9–10.
42. *Ibid.*, p. 14.
43. Henderson, p. iii.
44. Frederic Manning, *Her Privates We* (Hogarth Press, 1986; orig. 1929, as *The Middle Parts of Fortune*), p. 140.
45. *Ibid.*, p. 51.
46. *Ibid.*, p. 45.
47. Macdonald (1984), pp. 200 and 203.
48. Nettleingham (1917), p. 11.
49. John Brophy and Eric Partridge, *Songs and Slang of the British Soldier 1914–1918* (Eric Partridge, 1930), p. 4.
50. Giraud, p. 81.
51. For recent profiles of Henderson, see Raymond Ross, 'The Socialist Balladeer', *Times Educational Supplement*, 1 May 1987, and Murray Ritchie, 'Hymns to Heroes and a Treasury of Scottish Folklore', *Glasgow Herald*, 29 June 1987.
52. As note 43.
53. For details, see page 000.
54. Nettleingham (1918), p. 8.
55. Gavin Greig, *Folk Songs of the North-East* (Peterhead, *Buchan Observer*, 1914), art. 25, p. 2.
56. Coppard, pp. 6–7.
57. Anthony Boden, *F. W. Harvey: Soldier, Poet* (Alan Sutton, 1988), p. 153. Masefield's poem was originally entitled 'Captain Stratton's Fancy'.
58. Blackmore MS, p. 12.
59. Clive Branson, *British Soldier in India: The Letters of Clive Branson* (Communist Party, 1944), p. 12.

· NOTES ON SOURCES ·

The Army Alphabet
Blackmore MS, p. 33.

CHAPTER ONE – JOINING.
Kit Inspection
Blackmore MS, p. 2.

Join the British Army
Sung by Gordon Hall (Hall Tapes). Lottie Collins verse: Winstock, p. 213. Kilted soldiers verse: record, *The Blarney Folks' Ireland* (Emerald GES1084, 1968).

The Warwickshire RHA
Sung by Freda Palmer (who learnt it from a cousin who served in the First World War) of Witney, Oxfordshire, on the record, *When Sheepshearing's Done* (Topic 12T254, 1975). Reproduced here by permission of Mike Yates. For 'The Scarlet and the Blue', see Palmer, p. 59. For 'Off to Dublin in the Green' (IRA version), see record, *Dermot O'Brien* (Beltona SBE-R133, 1967).

Bungay Roger
Sung by Tony Hall of Norwich on the record, *The Larks They Sang Melodious* (Transatlantic XTRA XTRS 1141, 1974). 'The Awkward Recruit': street ballad without imprint (British Library, York Publications, BL 1870 c 2); reprinted in abbreviated form in A. Wyatt-Edgell (ed.), *A Collection of Soldiers' Songs* (London and Exeter, n.d.), no. 76. First World War version: 'Muddley Barracks', sung by Jumbo Brightwell on the record, *Songs from the Eel's Foot* (Topic 12TS261, 1975); printed in Palmer, p. 93. Recent version: under the title of 'The Yorkshire Blinder' on the cassette, *The Horkey Load*, vol. 2 (Veteran Tapes VT109, 1988).

Come On and Join
A. Mays (1986), pp. 78–80. B. Communicated by Hugh Anderson of Ascot Vale, Victoria, Australia, 1989. C. Sung by 'Nibs' Matthews (Matthews Tape).

Why Did We Join the Army?
Nettleingham (1917), no. 18. Air Force version: Ward-Jackson, p. 164. Version with tune: Giraud, p. 89.

I Don't Want to Join the Army
Sung by 'Nibs' Matthews (Matthews Tape). The singer, who spent 6½ years in the army, learnt this in 1939 as a marching song. He had a variant for the last line: 'And roger me foreskin away'. Brophy and Partridge (p. 59) include the song in the section 'rarely, if ever, sung on the march'. Nettleingham (1917), no. 19, gives the tune as 'Come, my lad and be a soldier'. Canadian version: Hopkins, p. 146.

We Are in Kitchener's Army/We are Fred Karno's Army
A. Frank Richards, *Old Soldiers Never Die* (with an introduction by Robert Graves, Faber, 1956; orig. 1933), p. 203. B. Stoke Tapes. Cf. 'Alley Sloper's Cavalree' and 'The Ragtime Navy': Nettleingham (1917), nos. 29 and 30; 'We are the Air-Sea Rescue': Ward-Jackson, pp. 17 and 174; and '10th MTB Flotilla Song': Tawney, no. 103.

Our Essex Camp
Nettleingham (1917), no. 40.
'Larkhill Camp': Page (1973), p. 50.

Orderly Song
Sung in 1986 by Malcolm Speake of Birmingham, who heard it from a fellow folk festival goer. Original text: *The Fellowship Song Book*, part 1, edited by Walford Davies (Curwen, 1915), no. 65. 'Solomon Levi': *The Scottish Students' Song Book* (2nd ed., 1897), p. 266.

Blandford in the Mud
Broadside without imprint (Royal Signals Museum, Blandford Camp, Dorset). 'Blandford Camp': same source.

The Rifle Brigade/The Gloucester Boys/The Buffs
A. Macdonald (1984), p. 139.
B. Sung by Jack Booth, Stroud, Glos.; recorded by Gwilym Davies, 1979.
C. Wilson, p. 50.
For a naval version, see Tawney, no. 112.

We Are the Kensington Boys/First Herts. Boys
A. Macdonald (1984), p. 31.
B. Sung by 'Nibs' Matthews (Matthews Tape).
'The Warwickshire Lads': Hewins, p. 135. 'The Guildford Boys': Newsletter, Regimental Association, Queen's Royal Surrey Regiment, no. 17 (May 1975), 8. 'Brummagem kids': Huggett, p. 35.

Here They Come
Wilson, p. 40.

I'll Never Forget the Day
Sung by John Gregson (Gregson Tape).
Second World War version: Page (1973), p. 31. WAAF version: Huggett, p. 148.

I Canna See the Target
Sung by Michael Grosvenor Myer of Haddenham, Cambs., 1987. The singer learned this in the late 1960s from Hubert Mitchell, who was a captain in the Black Watch during the Second World War. The tune, which is otherwise known as 'The Brown-haired Maiden', is in *Scots Guards' Standard Settings of Pipe Music* (Paterson's Publications, 5th ed., 1965), no. 14.

The Warwickshire Yeomanry
Page (1973), p. 54.
Godfrey anecdote: in his foreword to Hopkins, p. 11.

The Quartermaster Stores
Sung by Gordon Hall (Hall Tapes).
Winstock: p. 212. Spain: record, *Songs of the Spanish Civil War*, vol. 1 (Folkways FH5346, 1961).
Scatological version: de Witt, pp. 103–9. Canadian version: Hopkins, p. 85. Innocuous version: *Up in Arms*.

Any Complaints?
Seeger and MacColl, no. 63; *Bundook*.

Longmoor
Page (1973), p. 51.

I Wanna Go Home
Page (1976), p. 17.
Canadian versions: Hopkins, p. 76.

ATS Song
Page (1973), p. 155.

We Are the WAAFS
Sung by Margaret Gardham, Hull; recorded by Steve Gardham, 1982.

It Wasn't the WAAFs that Won the War
Communicated by Mrs Barbara Judge of Lincoln, 1987; learnt in Sheffield.
ATS version: Rex Gregson, private communication, 5 June 1989.

Stand by Your Beds
Sung by Michael Grosvenor Myer of Haddenham, Cambs., 1987. Learned during national service in the early 1950s.
Variant from Ted Poole of Swindon, Wilts., 1989. He was in the RAF from 1943 to 1947.

Stand on the Square
As previous item.

CHAPTER TWO – PUNISHMENT
Defaulters
Blackmore MS, p. 84.

McCaffery
Blackmore MS, p. 8.
Tom Langley: personal communication, 27 Sept. 1976. J. Imray: personal communication, 21 March 1980. Cyril Nuttall: personal communication, 30 Sept. 1977. John Gregson: Cox, p. 59. Roy Harris: record, *The Bitter and the Sweet* (Topic 12TS217, 1972), and in Palmer, p. 119. Gordon Hall: Hall Tapes. For further sung versions, see *Bundook* and record, Bob Davenport, *Postcards Home* (Topic 12TS318, 1977). For further information, see Palmer, 120–6.

The Reprieve
Communicated by Tom Langley of Birmingham, 1970.
For other instances of military clemency, see Palmer, pp. 112 ff.

Once to the Line
Sung by Bill House, Beaminster, Dorset; recorded by Nick and Mally Dow (cassettes, *Gin and Ale and Whisky*, OHC104, 1985, and *Diamonds in the Dew*, OHC108, 1986), by whose kind permission the text appears here.
'The Young Recruit': Palmer, p. 41, and record, *The Rambling Soldier* (Fellside FE017, 1979).

Yes, and We Can Do It
Giraud, p. 89.

Kevin Barry
Sung by John Gregson (Gregson Tape).
Cf. Colm O Lochlainn (ed.), *Irish Street Ballads* (Dublin, Three Candles, 1939), no. 49. The tune, 'Rolling Home', is in Roy Palmer (ed.), *The Oxford Book of Sea Songs* (Oxford University Press, 1986), no. 116. A second song on Barry, to the tune (like 'MacCaffery') of 'The Croppy Boy', begins: 'I've a sad but true story to relate' (see Patrick Galvin (ed.), *Irish Songs of Resistance* (Oak Publications, 1962, p. 67).

Lay Him Away O'er the Hillside
Walton's Treasury of Irish Songs and Ballads (Walton's Musical Instrument Galleries, 1943), p. 153. Cf. Cox, p. 60. 'More grooming': Cox, p. 61.

The Rambling Royal
Roy Palmer (ed.), *Everyman's Book of British Ballads* (Dent, 1980), no. 53. 'I am a real republican': P. W. Joyce (ed.), *Old Irish Folk Music and Songs* (Longmans, Green, 1909), vol. 3, no. 600. 'The Bold Belfast Shoemaker': O Lochlainn, *Irish Street Ballads*, no. 26.

Leopold Jail
Sung by Gordon Hall (Hall Tapes).

CHAPTER THREE – PRISONERS-OF-WAR
To a Dead Tommy
Stoke Tapes

The Kriegie Ballad
By Robert Garioch, in Victor Selwyn (ed.), *Poems of the Second World War* (Dent, 1985), p. 224. The text is reproduced here by permission of Hamish Henderson. For the tune, 'Botany Bay', see Hugh Anderson, *The Story of Australian Folksong* (New York, Oak Publications, 3rd ed., 1970), p. 4.

The Prisoner's Lament
By Dick Pavelin; sung by Bob Burt (Stoke Tapes).
The tune, 'Twenty-one Years in Dartmoor', can be heard on the cassette, *Charlie Carver* (Vintage Tapes, VT002, 1984).

The German Clockmaker
Stoke Tapes.
Cf. record, *Charlie Wills* (Leader LEA4041, 1972).

It Was in an Austrian Lager
Sung by Bob Burt (Stoke Tapes).
For the song 'Suvla Bay', of which this is a parody, see page 101.

Bella Ciao
Sung by Bill Arnitt, Jock Attrill, Frank Bayley and Jock Hamilton (Stoke Tapes).
See also A. Virgilio Savona and Michele L. Straniero, *Canti Della Resistenza Italiana* (Milan, Biblioteca Universale Rizzoli, 1985), no. 23.

Ringerangeroo
Stoke Tapes.
Cf. Hopkins, p. 140; Ewan MacColl and Peggy Seeger (eds.), *Travellers' Songs from England and Scotland* (Routledge, 1977), no. 40; record, *An English Folk Music Anthology* (Folkways FE38553, 1981).

They Say There's a Boat on the River
Stoke Tapes.
For a different version of the second verse, sung to the tune of 'My Bonny Lies Over the Ocean', see Mays (1969), p. 84.

The Gay Caballero
Stoke Tapes.
American version: Cray, p. 90. Cf. Coppard Tape.

Down the Mine
Written by Arthur Smith in Kinkaseki Camp, Taiwan. Communicated by Maurice Rooney of Norwich, 1990.

CHAPTER FOUR – SOLDIERING
(a) Before 1914
A Pontoon Wallah Goes Home
Blackmore MS, p. 132.

CRE Song
Sung by George Collinson, Hull; recorded by Steve Gardham, 1982.
Sailors' version: Stan Hugill, *Shanties from the Seven Seas* (Routledge, 1979), p. 425.

The Soldier's Return – I
Communicated by Maurice Ogg of Coleby, Lincs., who learnt it from Mrs Ruth Robinson (1880–1976) of Winteringham, Lincs.; published in Roy Palmer, 'Eight Songs Collected by Maurice Ogg', *English Dance and Song*, 43, no. 2 (1981), 9.

A British Soldier's Grave
Sung by the Copper family on the record, *A Song for Every Season* (Leader LEA4046, 1971). Reproduced here by permission of Bob Copper. Also published in Dallas, pp. 194–6.

Break the News to Mother
Sung by Mrs Lucy Woodall, Old Hill, Quarry Bank, Staffs.; recorded by Roy Palmer, 1970.
A very similar version, with music, is in Roy Palmer (ed.), *A Ballad History of England* (Batsford, 1979), no. 71.

Doin' My Duty
Sung by Ted Cobbin, Great Glemham, Norfolk; recorded by Keith Summers, 1973.

(b) The First World War
I Learned to Wash in Shell-holes
'Verses discovered in a dugout on the Western Front in 1918'; sent by V. E. Fagence to Newsletter, Regimental Association, Queen's Royal Surrey Regiment, no. 16 (November 1974), 11–12.

Grousing
Nettleingham (1917), no. 7.
Other versions: Brophy and Partridge, p. 39, and Winstock, pp. 242–3. 'Detrimental to good discipline': Nettleingham (1917), p. 26.

We Are but Little Seaforths Weak
Quoted under the title of 'Complaint of Our Private Soldiers' in Ewart MacIntosh's *War, the Liberator, and Other Pieces* (John Lane, 1918), p. 111. I am indebted to Lyn Macdonald for this text. The tune can be found in *The Methodist School Hymnal* (n.d.), no. 86.
Boer War version: Winstock, p. 243. Other First World War versions: Macdonald (1984), p. 135; Hewins, p. 134; Nettleingham (1917), no. 33. Cf. Tawney, no. 104 (sailors'); Ward-Jackson, p. 162 (airmen's); and Mays (1986), p. 49 (choirboys') versions.

We Beat 'em on the Marne
Brophy and Partridge, p. 39.

Neuve Chapelle
Sung by 'a street singer, ex-private of the Royal Iniskilling Fusiliers, Long Common, Coleraine'; noted by Sam Henry, 1933 (Belfast Public Library, Sam Henry Collection, no. 526; published also in Dallas, p. 220).
'Now a soldier's life': sung by Gordon Hall (Hall Tapes); learnt from his father who served in the First World War. Cf. Williamson, p. 135. 'Now old von Kluck': quoted in some extracts from Robert Graves' letters home, published anonymously in the *Spectator*, 11 Sept 1915, 320.

Suvla Bay
Sung by Gordon Hall (Hall Tapes).
Cf. cassette, *Diamonds in the Dew* (OHC 108, 1987). 'You can get arrested': Bill Scott (ed.), *The Second Penguin Australian Songbook* (Penguin, 1980), p. 171.

Salonika
Sung by Gordon Hall (Hall Tapes).
Cf. Tomas O Canainn (ed.), *Songs of Cork* (Gilbert Dalton, 1978), p. 60.

Never Mind
Giraud, pp. 49 and 96; collated with version sung by George Coppard (Coppard Tape).

Tickler's Jam
Sung by George Coppard (Coppard Tape).
Walter Bunn: interviewed by Roy Palmer, 1987.

Ode to Tickler
Nettleingham (1917), no. 8.

Plum and Apple
A. *Songs our Soldiers Sang* (n.d., n.p.), p. 16. This is claimed to have been written by Captain Arthur Eliot and J. P. Harrington, and composed by Herman Darewski. It is more likely that the words were merely remembered by Eliot and Harrington, and the tune arranged by Darewski.
B. From a sixpenny *Feldman's Song Book* (n.d., n.p.). Written and composed by Fred Fulton. Music published by Francis, Day and Hunter.
I am indebted for both copies to Adam McNaughtan of Glasgow.

Bully and Jam
By F. A. Todd, in *Sydney University Company Song Book* (Sydney, Australia, n.d.), pp. 15–16. The tune, 'Chantons l'Artillerie', is by Theodore Botrel. I am grateful to Hugh Anderson for sending me a copy of this song.

Fray Marie
Verse 1: Stoke Tapes; verse 2: Tawney, no. 102.
Antipodean version: Warren Fahey (ed.), *Eureka. Songs that Made Australia* (Omnibus Press, 1984), p. 230.

Three German Officers Crossed the Rhine
Sung by Gordon Hall (Hall Tapes).
Cf. Lomax, pp. 557 ff., and Hopkins, p. 139. Brophy and Partridge (p. 44) have a bowdlerised text.

I'll Be There
Giraud, p. 87.
Cf. Brophy and Partridge, p. 50. Blunden: *Undertones of War*, p. 142.

I Want to Go Home
Verse 1: Nettleingham (1917), no. 52; verse 2: Nettleingham (1918), p. 71. Cushing: unpublished interview with Lyn Macdonald. Robert Graves: *Goodbye to All That* (1960 ed.), p. 125. C. E. Montague: *Fiery Particles* (Chatto & Windus, 1930), p. 37. Williamson: p. 137. Ivor Gurney: *Stars in a Dark Night: The Letters of Ivor Gurney to the Chapman Family*, ed. Anthony Boden (Alan Sutton, 1986), p. 87. Dolph: p. 99. RAF version: Ward-Jackson, p. 231.

Ragtime Soldier
Sung by John Pearce, Birmingham; recorded by Roy Palmer, 1987. 'Any manifestation': Brophy and Partridge, p. 136. For a naval version, see Tawney, no. 18.

There's a Battalion out in France
Macdonald (1984), pp. 204–5.

The Soldier's Return – II
Sung by Willie Scott (1897–1989) of Hawick, who learnt it from his cousin, who in turn brought it back from the anonymous soldier who had composed it in the trenches during the First World

War. Published in Willie Scott, *Herd Laddie o the Glen. Songs of a Border Shepherd*, ed. by Alison McMorland (Tryst, 1988), p. 34. The tune can be found in James Kingsley (ed.), *Burns: Poems and Songs* (Oxford University Press, 1969), no. 392.

Hanging on the Old Barbed Wire
Sung by Gordon Hall (Hall Tapes).
Lyn Macdonald: *The Roses of No Man's Land* (Macmillan, 1984 ed.), p. 178. First World War versions: Brophy and Partridge, pp. 53–4; Dolph, pp. 87–9; Lomax, p. 555. David Jones: *In Parenthesis* (Faber, 1937), part 5. J. B. Priestley: *Margin Released* (Heinemann, 1962), p. 111. Canadian version: Hopkins, p. 90. For a version on record, see Bob Davenport, *Postcards Home* (Topic 12T318, 1977). The 'latrine' suggestion was made by John Hetherington of Birmingham among his manuscript annotations to the second (1930) edition of Brophy and Partridge. The copy is now in the War Poetry Collection at Birmingham Reference Library.

The Boys of Palestine
Nettleingham (1918), pp. 26–7.

Oh! It's a Lovely War
Giraud, p. 77.
Cf. Dolph, p. 143.

The Last Long Mile
Nettleingham (1918), pp. 40–2.
Cf. Giraud, p. 83.

Soldier's Lullaby
Communicated by Mrs Barbara Hardy, Ormskirk, Lancs., 1987; learnt from her mother.
Cf. Patrick MacGill, *Soldier Songs*, p. 13; Brophy and Partridge, p. 51 (as 'Far, far from Ypres').

I Wore a Tunic
Sung by Gordon Hall (Hall Tapes).
Brophy and Partridge: p. 41. Cf. copy with music, in Giraud, p. 91.

Old Joe Whip
Sung by Jackie Booth, Stroud, Glos.; recorded by Gwilym Davies, 1979.
'The Brave Grenadier': Dolph, p. 180.

When this Poxy War is Over
Sung by Gordon Hall (Hall Tapes).
Cf. Brophy and Partridge, p. 50; Hopkins, p. 103 (Canadian version from Second World War); Ward-Jackson, p. 13 (RFC version). Records: *Up in Arms*, *Bundook* and *Postcards Home*.

(c) Between the Wars
Goodbye, India
Blackmore MS, p. 99.

Shaibah Blues
Sung by George Collinson, Hull; recorded by Steve Gardham, 1982.
Cf. Ward-Jackson, p. 94.

Hold Your Row
Ward-Jackson, pp. 92–3.

The Artillery Alphabet
Text in the Royal Artillery Institution, Woolwich. I am indebted to Steve Gardham for the copy. A tune can be found in Gardham's book, *An East Riding Songster* (Lincolnshire and Humberside

Arts, 1982), no. 31, and also, under the title of 'The Sailor's Alphabet', in Palmer, *Oxford Book of Sea Songs*, no. 107. Canadian version: Hopkins, p. 70. RAC version: communicated by Joe Hodgson of Preston, 1987.

Merry Battery Boys
Sung by John Gregson (Gregson Tape).

Sixteen Annas, One Rupee
Sung by John Gregson (Gregson Tape).
'Bombay Bibley': Page (1973), p. 205.

Orderly Man
Sung by John Gregson (Cox, pp. 58–9).
'If you're doing seven years': Cox, p. 60.

A Soldier's Farewell to India
Communicated by Harold Wirdnam of Newent, Glos., 1989.
Cf. Blackmore MS, p. 112.

Cut Down
Blackmore MS, p. 9.
'The Buck's Elegy': John Holloway and Joan Black (eds), *Later English Broadside Ballads* (Routledge, 1975), no. 17. Hewins version: text in Hewins, p. 46; with tune in *English Dance and Song*, 43, no. 3 (1981), 13. Cavalry version: Mays (1969), p. 42.
Cf. Hopkins, p. 119; Ward-Jackson, p. 2; Tawney, no. 101; Winstock, p. 244. Record: *Bundook*.

The Codfish
Sung by George A. Bregenzer, Hayes, Middlesex, on tape privately communicated, 1987.
'The Sea Crabb': *Bishop Percy's Folio Manuscript. Loose and Humorous Songs*, ed. by Frederick J. Furnivall (1868), p. 99. See also Guthrie T. Meade, 'The Sea Crab', *Mid-West Folklore*, 8 (1958), 91–100. 'Tee, I, Ee, I, O': Nettleingham (1918), p. 28. Record: *Across the Western Ocean* (Swallowtail St4, 1973), under the title of 'The Crayfish'.

Chilli of Chowringhee
Sung by Bill ('Pop') Hingston on the cassette, *Hingston's Half-hour* (People's Stage Tapes 03, n.d.).
See Sam Richards, 'Bill Hingston – a Biography in Song', *Oral History*, 10, no. 1 (1982), 24–46.

The Valley of Jarama
Frank Ryan (ed.), *XV International Brigade* (Commissariat of War, XV Brigade, 1975), p. 97.
'Was sung in many versions': Bill Alexander, interview, 1986; see also his book, *British Volunteers for Liberty: Spain 1936–39* (Lawrence and Wishart, 1982).

Bless 'em All
Stoke Tapes.
Winstock: p. 212. Ward-Jackson: p. 22. Sailors: Tawney, no. 107. Paratroops, bombers, coastal command: Ward-Jackson, pp. 136–7. Canadians: Hopkins, p. 105. Americans: Cray, pp. 146–7 and 195–8. Records: *Bundook*, *Up in Arms*.

(d) The Second World War
A Soldier's Catechism
Blackmore MS, pp. 47–8.
The manuscript has some damage, and gaps have been filled from a version printed in Charles Hindley, *Curiosities of Street Literature* (1871), p. 90. For more recent versions, see *Up in Arms* and Page (1976), p. 15.

The Digger's Song
Scott, *Second Penguin Australian Songbook*, p. 169.
Cf. Page (1973), p. 136 (as 'Horseferry Lane') and Cray, pp. 175–6.

In Bloody Orkney
Original text: broadsheet headed 'Life in the Orkneys' (Orkney Archives, Kirkwall, D31/3/2/19);
published in *Verse and Worse*, ed. A. Silcock (1952), pp. 251–2.
Cf. Ward-Jackson, p. 167; Page (1973), p. 52; *Up in Arms.*

The Royal Artillery
Page (1973), p. 200.

Soldier and Sailor
A. Sung by Nibs Matthews, 1986 (Matthews Tape). Verse 5, which he declined to sing, on the
grounds that it was 'too crude', has been added from the singing of Pop Hingston, from the
cassette, *Hingston's Half-hour.*
B. Sung by Mr May, Birmingham; recorded by Roy Palmer, 1970. Other versions: Ward-Jackson,
p. 133 ('The Airman's Prayer'); Tawney, no. 92 ('A Matelot and a Pongo'); *Cecil Sharp's Collection
of English Folk Songs*, ed. Maud Karpeles (Oxford University Press, 1974), no. 276. Street ballad:
printed by H. P. Such of London (British Library, Crampton Collection, 11621 h 11, vol. 5,
p. 46). Boer War: Winstock, p. 243. Canadian version: Hopkins, pp. 194 and 44.

How Did I Ever Become a Corporal?
Communicated by Rex Gregson of Carlisle, 1989. Gregson served in the Royal Signals during the
Second World War.

Roll Me Over
Sung by Gordon Hall (Hall Tapes).
Chelsea Pensioners: Winstock, p. 212. Canadian version: Hopkins, p. 135.

Lulu
Sung by Nibs Matthews (Matthews Tape); learnt, 1939–41.
Transatlantic versions: Cray, pp. 54–6; Dolph, pp. 93–4; Hopkins, p. 159.

How Ashamed I Was
Sung by Nibs Matthews (Matthews Tape).
Canadian versions: Hopkins, pp. 133 and 82.

Watch and Chain Song
Sung by Nibs Matthews (Matthews Tape).
Cf. Cray, p. 92.

The Army Dance
Page (1976), pp. 101–2.
Naval version: Palmer, *Oxford Book of Sea Songs*, no. 147. Frank Richards: see his book *Old Soldier
Sahib* (Faber, 1936), p. 25.

Died for Love
Sung by Gordon Hall (Hall Tapes).
Cf. Cox, p. 62; Henderson, p. 44; Ward-Jackson, p. 126; Stoke Tapes.

The Merry Month of May
Ward-Jackson, pp. 242–3.

Paratrooper's Song
Sung by members of the RNR at a social evening in Birmingham; recorded by Roy Palmer, 1984.
For a Canadian version, see Hopkins, p.123.

This Old Coat of Mine
Sung by George Collinson, Hull; recorded by Steve Gardham, 1982. One soldier's account: Stan
McMahon, personal communication, 10 March 1987. Other versions: Cox, p. 63; Ward-Jackson,
p. 113. Midshipman's logbook: Tawney, p. 132. Record: *The Watersons* (Topic 12T142, 1966), as
'All For Me Grog'.

On the Move
Ward-Jackson, pp. 162–3.
Bundook.

The Ballad of Wadi Maktilla
Henderson, pp. 7–8.
Bundook.

The Song of the 258 General Transport
Page (1973), p. 73.

My Little Dugout in the Sand
Communicated by Rex Gregson of Carlisle, 1989.
Cf. Page (1973), p. 70, where the tune is given as 'Leaning on a Lamppost'.

Never Go to Mersa
Page (1976), p. 52.

Seven Years in the Sand
Seeger and MacColl, no. 69; *Bundook.*

Fucking Tobruk
Page (1973), p. 93.

Shari Wag El Burka
Page (1973), p. 83.

The Streets of Minturno
Sung by Donald Mitchell, Stroud, Glos.; recorded by Gwilym Davies, 1979.

The Highland Division's Farewell to Sicily
Henderson, pp. 15–16, with two small changes subsequently adopted by the author. 'Best song':
Norman Buchan (ed.), *101 Scottish Songs* (Collins, 1962), p. 155. *Bundook.*

Ballad of Anzio
Henderson, pp. 43–4.

D-Day Dodgers
Written by Lance-Sergeant Harry Pynn; communicated by his widow, Mrs Evelyn Pynn, Crick,
Northants, 1987.
Lady Astor verses: Selwyn, *Poems of the Second World War*, p. 237; unpublished version, sung by
Jackie Booth of Stroud, Glos., and recorded by Gwilym Davies, 1977; Ward-Jackson, p. 235.
Desert version of 'Lili Marlene': Huggett, p. 143. A Canadian version of 'D-Day Dodgers' is in
Hopkins (p. 110), together with 'Onwards to the Po' (p. 111), another song of the Italian
campaign, to the same tune. Records: *Bundook, Up in Arms* and *The Spinners by Arrangement* (EMI
EMC3009, 1973).

South of Meiktila
Written by Sergeant Tommy Wren (Border Regiment Museum, Carlisle, typescript). For 'South
of Colombo' and 'South of the Sangro', see Hopkins, pp. 83 and 93.

The Dying Soldier
A. Border Regiment Museum, Carlisle, typescript entitled 'Bury me out in the jungle'. B. Airborne Forces Museum, Aldershot. Booklet entitled *Parachutist Song Hits*, no. 12, p. 4. Cf. Page (1973), p. 203, and *Bundook*.

Africa Star
Ward-Jackson, pp. 225–7.

Discharge Song
Communicated by Hugh Anderson, Ascot Vale, Victoria, Australia, 1989. Cf. Page (1973), p. 227.

I Don't Want My Name on a Cenotaph
Page (1976), p. 20.

The '39–'45 Star
Communicated by Walter Pardon of Knapton, Norfolk, 1986. Walter Pardon served in the army during the Second World War.

(e) After 1945
Roll on the Boat
Blackmore MS, p. 97.

Spud Spedding's Broken Boys
Border Regiment Museum, Carlisle, typescript.

The Minden Dandies
Same source.

Moving On
Tony McCarthy (ed.), *Bawdy British Folk Songs* (Wolfe, 1972), pp. 77–8.

Ghost Army of Korea
Seeger and MacColl, no. 68; *Bundook*.
'We've Done our Hitch in Hell': Lomax, p. 554. See also, 'A Pontoon Wallah Goes Home' (page 89).

Seven Nights Drunk
Sung by Gordon Hall (Hall Tapes).
'Our Goodman': Francis James Child, *The English and Scottish Popular Ballads* (Boston, 1882–98), no. 274.

The REME Song
Composite text made up of verses supplied by David Blick of Newent, Glos., who served in the REME in Germany in the late 1950s, Staff-Sergeant Townley (who wrote verse 4 himself), Corporal Brooking and others currently serving in the REME (letters, 1989). I am indebted to Mr B. S. Baxter, Deputy Curator of the REME Museum, Arborfield, for his help with this item.

The Soldier
Written by Harvey Andrews, and issued on Beeswing Records KLBEE002, 1972. I am indebted to Harvey Andrews and to Lyn Macdonald for further information about the song.

Now that You're an Army Wife
Written by Liz Boden and Gaynor Bream, 1988, with assistance from Mr E. People. I am grateful to Marie Thomas for drawing my attention to the song.

· ACKNOWLEDGEMENTS ·

I should like to thank all the singers, authors, collectors and editors, and also the staffs of institutions listed in the Sources. In addition, I should like to express my gratitude to Raphael Samuel (for suggesting that I take on this project), Pat Palmer (for musical advice), E. V. ('Andy') Anderson, L. Baars, Phyl Blamire, Major F. W. G. Brodrick, Lieutenant-Colonel P. Burdick (Devonshire and Dorset Regiment), Roger Cleverley, Bob Copper, Mrs Olive Craig, Tony Davis, R. P. Graves, Mrs E. Gregson, Keith Gregson, A. L. Griffiths, Barbara Hardy, Geoffrey Hewitt ('Folk on 2'), Mrs F. L. Hingston, Norman Holme (Regimental Museum, Royal Welch Regiment), Harry Hopkins, D. T. Hughes, Eileen Marino (BBC Radio WM), Lieutenant-Colonel R. K. May (Regimental Museum, Border Regiment), Stan McMahon, Maurie Milner (Imperial War Museum), Douglas Miller, Tony Newing (*The Globe and Laurel*), Cyril Nuttall, Arthur Padgett, Simon Palmer, Major R. B. and Mrs Olga Patch, Gordon B. Perks, Lieutenant-Colonel J. Petty, Stephen Price (Birmingham Museum and Art Gallery), Evelyn Pynn, C. W. Rowley, Charles Seaton (the *Spectator*), Mrs Elizabeth Spedding, Keith Summers, Cyril Tawney, F. G. Woodrough (Queen's Royal Surrey Regimental Museum) and Mike Yates.

For permission to reprint copyright material I should like to thank for songs: Harvey Andrews and Westminster Music Ltd ('The Soldier'); International Music Publications ('Any Complaints?', 'Ghost Army of Korea' and 'Seven Years in the Sand'); and for illustrations: Aberdeen Journals (p. 40), Airborne Forces Museum (pp. 184–5), Bill Alexander (p. 141), (the illustrations on pp. 32, 37, 107, 116, 119, 123, 125 and 134 are from my own collection), Cookworthy Museum, Kingsbridge, Devon (pp. 26 and 34), Leo Cooper (p. 64), S. R. Earle (p. 74), Gloucestershire Regiment Museum (pp. 39, 94 and 195–6), Mrs E. Gregson (p. 132), Rex Gregson (pp. 168–9), Gordon Hall (p. 44), Hamish Henderson (p. 176), Angela Hewins (p. 114), Mrs F. L. Hingston (p. 188), John Howson (p. 105), Hulton Picture Company (p. 31), Imperial War Museum (pp. 50, 97, 148–50, 175, 181 and 187), T. M. Jones (p. 78), The King's Own Royal Border Regiment Museum (pp. 90, 193), *The Navy and Army Illustrated* (pp. 23, 28 (upper), 42 and 143), Mrs E. Pynn (p. 179), Mrs E. Smith (pp. 70 and 76) and Harold Wirdnam (pp. 28 (lower), 129, 136–7 and 161). The source of the photographs on pp. 127, 159 and 162 is Frank Huggett (see Abbreviations), whom it has not been possible to trace.

· GLOSSARY·

ackers and tosh: bread and cheese

adjutant: officer (usually a captain) responsible for regimental organisation, and discipline of junior officers

acker: a coin; hence 'akkers' or 'ackers', money

Alleyman: German

ANZAC: Australian and New Zealand Army Corps

Arbeit: work

ASC: Army Service Corps (later RASC)

ATS: [Women's] Auxiliary Territorial Service (later WRAC, Women's Royal Army Corps)

Aufstehen: stand up

basha: dugout

Bauer: farmer, peasant

billets: accommodation

bint: woman

blanco: preparation (usually buff in colour) spread on webbing

Blighty: England

bluchers: boots

bobajee: cook

buckshee: free, spare

bully (beef): corned beef (from '*boeuf bouilli*')

bundu: desert

calico, bits of: women

CB: confined to barracks

CC: confined to camp (RAF version of CB)

char: tea

chung: dry river bed

C in C: commander-in-chief

civvies: civilian clothes

civvy street: civilian life

CO: commanding officer

CRE: Corps of Royal Engineers

cushy: easy, comfortable

dhobi wallah: laundry man

digger: private, mate, or Australian in general

Eighty-eights: 88 mm guns; or Junkers 88 'planes

ENSA: Entertainment National Services Association (provided entertainment for the services during the Second World War)

Eyetie: Italian

fatigues: tasks such as peeling potatoes, cleaning cooking equipment, picking up litter, delivering coal (sometimes routine work, sometimes awarded as punishment)

fire-step: ledge in trench on which men mounted in order to fire weapons, or from which to advance

flea-pit: bed

four-by-two: piece of flannel, four inches by two, which was soaked in oil and pulled through a rifle barrel on a cord (called a 'pull-through') in order to clean it

Gefangener: prisoner

glasshouse: military prison

gong: medal

housewife: small cloth pouch holding needles, thread and wool

Jack Johnsons: heavy shells (from boxer of same name)

jankers: CB

Kriegie = Kriegsgefangener: prisoner-of-war

KD: khaki drill (cloth)

KRR: King's Royal Rifle Corps

LAD: Light Aid Detachment

Lager: prison camp

lance-jack: lance-corporal

Maconochie: tinned stew (from maker's name)

maknoon: mad

matlow: sailor

MG: machine gun

mob: unit, regiment

MP: military policeman

NAAFI: Navy, Army and Air Force Institutes (organisation with provides canteen facilities for services)

naik: corporal

napoo: finished, no good

Nip: Japanese

orderly: soldier working on particular task (e.g. post orderly, dining room orderly, medical orderly)

orderly man: soldier appointed to fetch meals or do other menial tasks, in addition to his normal duties

orderly officer, sergeant, etc.: one selected by rota to perform certain inspections and duties on a particular day

orderly room: administrative offices of regiment; place where CO tries men for regimental offences

Ox. and Bucks.: Oxfordshire and Buckinghamshire Light Infantry

pack-drill: drill, performed as punishment, in full marching order, including heavy pack and rifle

pani: sea

peechi: soon

Posten: sentry

POW: prisoner-of-war

provost-sergeant: sergeant in charge of regimental police (first word pronounced 'provo')

pull-through: cord used to pull cleaning four-by-two (*qv*) through rifle

pusser = purser: naval officer responsible for issue of clothing and provisions (proverbial for meanness)

quarter-bloke = quartermaster-sergeant: person responsible for issue of clothing, equipment and bedding

RA: Royal Artillery

RAC: Royal Armoured Corps

RAMC: Royal Army Medical Corps (popularly known as Rob All My Comrades)

RE: Royal Engineers

redcap: military policeman (as opposed to regimental policeman)

reveille: signal for time for getting up (pronounced 'revally')

RFA: Royal Field Artillery

RFC: Royal Flying Corps

RHA: Royal Horse Artillery

rooti-gong: long service medal

rough-riding: breaking in and training of horses

RP: regimental policeman

sangar: small breastwork or rifle pit, often constructed of boulders grouped round a natural hollow

SHQ: squadron headquarters (in RAF)

small kit: small pack, containing pyjamas, towel and shaving kit, which had to be carried when reporting sick

solid: stupid person

Soldier's Friend: brass polish

SP: station policeman (RAF)

squaddy: ordinary soldier

square: barrack square, parade ground

stand-to: prepare to go into action

sub = subaltern: lieutenant or second-lieutenant

swaddy: ordinary soldier

swish: ? butter

TA: Territorial Army

tattoo: signal for lights-out

tedeschi: Germans

TEWTs: Tactical Exercises Without Troops

ticket: discharge papers

Tickler: manufacturer of jam

tosh: ? cheese

trog: food

Vickers men: machine gunners

WAAC: Women's Auxiliary Army Corps, or a member of it

WAAF: Women's Auxiliary Air Force, or a member of it

wad: sandwich

wallah: man

whizzbang: light shell

WO I: warrant officer, class I

WRAF: Women's Royal Air Force

Wren(s) = WRNS: Women's Royal Naval Service, or (a) member(s) of it

ᏯᎶ · INDEX OF SONG TITLES, · ᏯᎶ
· TUNE TITLES AND FIRST LINES ·

References in bold type after titles indicate that a text is printed at that point.